CM00741062

SUN GOD
Moon Maiden

ABOUT AUTHOR

Gordon Strong is a writer, speaker, and workshop host. He is well-known in the U.K. and the West Coast of America. He has published several books on myths, magic and sacred monuments and numerous novels. Music, laughter with friends, and walking are his other pursuits. He lives in Somerset. Gordon on how he would describe his writing:

"When I write about metaphysics I'm bringing in quantum, neurology, cosmology and philosophy simply because they are part of the picture. I'm a believer in balancing reason and the intuition so as to get the best out of both qualities. In my fiction I'm upholding the traditional virtues of nobility and respect and above all, love. I champion the individual against the corporate mindless monster, very much a theme of our times. I'm not a cynic, but I'm not so much of a romantic either that I drift off into Fluffyland. I'm funny too, humour is part of awareness."

SUN GOD
Moon Maiden

Gordon Strong

Chicago, Illinois

Sun God & Moon Maiden: The Secret World of the Holy Grail copyright © 2023 by Gordon Strong. All rights reserved. No part of this book may be reproduced in any manner whatsoever without written permission from Crossed Crow Books, except in the case of brief quotations embodied in critical articles and reviews.

First Edition.
First Printing, 2023.

ISBN: 978-1-959883-14-2
Library of Congress Control Number: 2023935781

Cover design by Leonardo Avila.
Typesetting by Lindsay Mathers.
Edited by Becca Fleming.

Disclaimer: Crossed Crow Books, LLC does not participate in, endorse, or have any authority or responsibility concerning private business transactions between our authors and the public. Any internet references contained in this work were found to be valid during the time of publication, however, the publisher cannot guarantee that a specific reference will continue to be maintained. This book's material is not intended to diagnose, treat, cure, or prevent any disease, disorder, ailment, or any physical or psychological condition. The author, publisher, and its associates shall not be held liable for the reader's choices when approaching this book's material. The views and opinions expressed within this book are those of the author alone and do not necessarily reflect the views and opinions of the publisher.

Published by:
Crossed Crow Books, LLC
6934 N Glenwood Ave, Suite C
Chicago, IL 60626
www.crossedcrowbooks.com

Printed in the United States of America.

To Alan Richardson who showed me magick.

CONTENTS

Introduction.............................. 1

1.   Holy Vessel.............................. 3

II.   God and Goddess........................ 19

III.   Sun God................................. 33

IV.   The Quest.............................. 43

V.   Altered States........................ 53

VI.   Cosmic Time........................... 67

VII.   All in Parallel...................... 77

VIII.   Moon Maiden.......................... 93

IX.   Dark Day............................. 105

X.   Aquarian Age......................... 119

Appendix—King Arthur: The
Wasteland & the New Age.......... 127

Endnotes............................... 177

Bibliography.......................... 195

INTRODUCTION

No thesis involving the Grail can be anything but speculation—its very nature almost demands it. As civilization moves ever more rapidly—hopefully towards a greater enlightenment—and if the pieces of the cosmic puzzle fit into place, then the Holy of Holies will be revealed.

The purpose of the Grail is to create form, whether spiritual or material. The divine gestation occurs when the essentially Watery nature of the vessel is united with cardinal Fire. The latter is symbolized in, among other things, the questing knight. When the divine union he is seeking occurs, then the lance is wedded to the cup for all eternity.

The reasoning mind prefers to group knowledge into particular disciplines—physics, metaphysics, history, myth, and so on. An attempt has been made in these pages to show that it is possible to demonstrate a synthesis of the many, and sometimes disparate, ideas that surround the Holy Vessel.

As our study progresses, we celebrate the divine power of man and woman. It is our desire to explore the ways in which we perceive ourselves regarding the universe. What is our place in it and how does the cosmos regard us? In our "consciousness," every possibility exists and this limitless potential is at the centre of our study.

In the Quest lies the tale of every man and woman's journey to gain enlightenment. The Grail saga has resonated through the ages and is reflected, more than we may realise, in our own times.

Gordon Strong
Portishead, England
September 2010

I. HOLY VESSEL

"PARSIFAL:
WHAT IS THE GRAIL?

GURNEMANZ:
I MAY NOT SAY:
BUT IF TO SERVE IT THOU BE BIDDEN,
KNOWLEDGE OF IT WILL BE HIDDEN—AND LO!

PARSIFAL:
ME THINKS I KNOW THEE NOW INDEED,
NO EARTHLY ROAD TO IT DOTH LEAD,
BY NO ONE CAN IT BE DETECTED
WHO BY ITSELF IS NOT ELECTED."

— WOLFRAM VON ESCHENBACH

The Grail has been a source of fascination to historians, poets, and pilgrims for nearly a thousand years. Chretien de Troyes, a French poet of the twelfth century, more or less invented the image that we have come to associate with the holy vessel. His vision was the modern prototype. Ironically perhaps, Chretien wrote the *Conte du Graal* but never completed it. That task was undertaken by Wolfram Von Eschenbach, who adapted Chretien's original notion to link the Grail with the Ark of the Covenant. The reasons for doing this are perfectly understandable—both are made of gold and both possess a radiance emanating from a fiery celestial energy.

The edict that only the pure may engage with such a holy object arrived with the Christianization of the Grail. In the tales of an earlier era, the ethos is very different. In a similar saga originating from India, the vessel is stolen by the leader of the adventurers. He may be Sayed

Khidr Rumi Khapradri, who is sometimes referred to as "the Cup Bearer of Turkestan." In other versions, a hero or chieftain obtains the cauldron/Grail and returns with it to his people. For instance, the Irish hero Cuchulainn harrows hell and returns in triumph with his prize.

A customary feature of these early accounts is that the guardian of the treasure must be a dragon or some other fearsome creature. The hero must somehow outwit his adversary—one that seems mightier than himself, even unconquerable. Is this an allegory, that man must first subdue his lower nature in order to gain enlightenment?

Other sacred artefacts through the ages have included a book (many of the sacred texts of the East are considered to be holy articles), a mirror (part of the Japanese regalia), and a nail (perhaps from the True Cross). The outward appearance of the object is less important than the reverence afforded to it—the very "presence." The poet and the seeker know only too well of this quality. Stephen Coote, writing of the poet Keats, mentions,

> "...that visionary power of the poet whereby his delight in the physical world is transformed through his imagination into an intimation of eternal truth and beauty, those 'essences'...whose power over the inner self gives them an aura of the divine."[1]

Ark of the Covenant

We have already mentioned the Ark of the Covenant and its relationship to the Grail. Concerning this, Graham Hancock's thesis is interesting but not wholly convincing. He proposes that Wolfram von Eschenbach, when writing of the Grail in *Parsifal*, may have been using the term as a kind of cipher for the Ark. The strongest piece of evidence Hancock cites concerns the "Grail Question." Assessing the version of these events depicted by Eschenbach, Hancock comes to an original conclusion. He claims that the "question" is more oracular than transformative.

> "We fell on our knees before the Grail, where suddenly we saw it written that a knight would come to us and were he heard to ask a question there, our sorrows would be at an end...if he asks his question in season he shall have the Kingdom."[2]

It is known that the Ark was, like the Oracle at Delphi, consulted by those seeking divine guidance, but the meaning of the quoted text is certainly ambiguous. Is "the Kingdom" mentioned a reference to the "Kingdom of God"? By embracing that state, is all knowledge and understanding gained? Or is this a reference to the Waste Land and the power to make that land whole once more? Whatever Eschenbach's intentions, we may only conclude that tales of "questing" are often remarkably similar.

In the twelfth century when the sacred cup became a Christian symbol, it was associated exclusively with the Eucharist. To the medieval mind, the Grail, the figure of the Virgin Mary, and the Ark were inseparably associated, and the imagery used to depict them was almost interchangeable. Eschenbach associated the virtue of grace with the Grail and, unusual for the times, he advocated understanding between different religious faiths. The Crusades then being at their bloodiest heights, religious tolerance would probably not have been a popular stance.

Magick Cauldron

The goddess figures that appear in the Celtic canon are many and fascinating. As the mythological thread is woven over the centuries, Welsh and Irish divinities begin to intermingle. It is here that occurs the first mention of an "enchantress"—*Cerridwen.* She was the wife of *Tegid Voel,* a bald giant who lived in a world beneath a lake. In myth, the connection between water and otherworldly powers is rife.

The "original Grail" was the Celtic "Cauldron of Cerridwen." This object possessed supernatural powers and was capable of providing both material and spiritual sustenance to those who requested it. An ability to recite original verse—the bardic tradition—was a talent held in high regard among the Celtic races and the cauldron gave inspiration to poets. In another guise, the cauldron was a scrying bowl—one that divined the future.

The celebrated *Gundestrup Cauldron* has enigmatic designs engraved upon it. Cernunnos, the "Lord of all Animals" is shown in majesty, his stag's horns representing Fire and virility. He also evokes the ecstasy associated with intoxication. Achieving an altered state is a method of gaining entry into the otherworld (a theme we shall investigate in some detail in our study). Another tableau depicts a column of warriors marching, apparently willingly, to be sacrificed. Another troop, reborn after their immersion in the cauldron, is seen marching away from us, presumably to enjoy a finer life.

The sacrifice that the universe demands from the seeker upon the path is the death of the self. The concept of a willing sacrifice is somewhat alien to a modern generation, exposed as they have been to a "me first" attitude. Cultural influences which uphold "self-expression" and the cult of personality have been paramount since the middle of the twentieth century.

To the ancients, it would have been unquestionably accepted that the gods demanded sacrifices—the notion might seem repugnant to modern man. It is often difficult for us to fully understand the belief systems that brought this practice to the fore. For a man to be chosen as a sacrifice was once considered a great honour as it meant that the gods guaranteed him immortality. To die in battle was considered to have the same honour.

The warrior consciousness is akin to the seeker. Both strive to see the ultimate truth in whatever they experience. The Arthurian tales have their essence in the cult of sacrifice, and we shall see how this idea manifests itself for the King and his knights. The warrior is unlike other men, for he is ready to cast aside all material considerations in his pursuit of glory. What is this thing—glory? As well as "exalted renown," the O.E.D. gives as a definition— "state of exaltation" and "splendour of heaven."

This warrior's view is expounded further in the philosophy of Carlos Castaneda, the chronicler of the exploits of the Yaqui shaman Don Juan. The sorcerer graphically demonstrates the mechanics of perception to his rather gauche pupil. To this end, Don Juan encourages him to abandon the habitual way in which he perceives the world and begin to see things anew. He must learn to "stop the world," and when he does, so he will experience extraordinary shifts in the nature of reality. The apparent ability to project the physical self at great distances, see fantastic creatures, and know intimately the ways of creation—these are all part of this radical new way of "seeing."

The Cup

With its Christianization came a view of the Grail as a symbol of transcendence. It became the goal of many a spiritual pilgrimage, a way of experiencing Christ. The conviction that the Grail is either the cup used at the Last Supper or the cup in which Joseph of Arimathea collected the blood of Christ at the crucifixion is the foundation of the Grail "myth." Of its history—the whereabouts of an actual object through the ages—little has been recorded. The Grail story does not occur in myths east of Germany, with one exception.

> *"In Persian tradition a similar miraculous and mystical vessel was given to Jamshid, the pattern of perfect kings, in whose reign the Golden Age was realized in Iran. He was the favourite of Ormuzd and his legitimate representative on earth; he discovered the 'Goblet of the Sun' when digging the foundation of Persepolis, and from him it passed to Alexander the Great. It is a symbol of the world."[3]*

It must be said that accounts of several objects, all supposedly the "Grail," have emerged over the centuries. In 711, with the Arab conquest of Toledo came rumours that the Muslims were in possession of "Solomon's Treasure." Solomon's Temple was located in Jerusalem and once housed the Ark of the Covenant. As we have learned, references to the "Grail" and the "Ark of the Covenant" may be to the same object.

The Grail was not the only sanctified treasure sought by the English king and crusader Richard the Lionheart. In 1187, Saladin removed the Holy Sepulcher and the "fragment of the True Cross" from Jerusalem. It was the recovery of these objects, seen as tremendous icons of the Christian faith, that had initially spurred the Crusades. Proposing an extraordinary morality, the Church promised to give total absolution for sins committed by any crusading knight. What this meant was tacit approval of wholesale slaughter and rape in the so-called Holy Land.

Other claims in different parts of the world were made for certain treasures being the "true" Grail. The Emerald Chalice at Genoa (later discovered to be made of green glass) and the agate cup in the

Cathedral of Valencia are two of the most celebrated examples. The silver "Antioch Cup," discovered after World War I, was another contender. This was later found to date from the sixth century and had originally been designed as a lamp. Of locations for the Grail— The Rosslyn Chapel in Scotland, a church in Aberystwyth in Wales, and the Chalice Well in Glastonbury—all have been suggested at different times.

Quite the most intriguing tale concerns that known as the *Nanteos Cup*. It is said that the cup was turned on a lathe in the Nazareth carpenter's workshop by Jesus himself.[4] The function of such a vessel may have been quite mundane—as a drinking vessel for the Saviour to take with him on his journeys in that later period of his life; or indeed, it may have served a more sacred purpose as the vessel used at the Last Supper.

Whatever its purpose, this was the cup that Joseph of Arimathea brought with him to Britain and thence to Glastonbury. The vessel was among the treasures of the monks of Glastonbury Abbey. At the Dissolution of the Monasteries, a group of seven monks, including the prior, fled with the cup into Wales. Their intended refuge was Strata Florida Abbey in Cardiganshire. Unfortunately, they were pursued, and so the monks took to the hills and reached Nanteos House near Aberystwyth.

There, the prior became chaplain to Mr. Powell, the owner, and the other monks became servants on his estate. As the seven gradually died off, the last remaining monk revealed that they possessed the Grail. The treasure was then given into the keeping of the Powell family "until the church shall claim her own." The family duly guarded the cup for the next four hundred years.

This remarkable tale then becomes even more so when one learns that the cup effected cures to those who desired to benefit from its singular powers. A record was kept of the loaning of the cup by the butler in the early nineteenth century. That indefatigable polymath Lionel Fanthorpe has perused the book which contains the details of these accounts. He describes them as being written in "the most beautiful copperplate." Lionel has also handled the cup and remarked upon the dark appearance of the wood.

And what of the appearance of the Nanteos Cup? It seems originally to have been six to eight inches in height but has been reduced in size by too-ardent pilgrims biting off pieces of the wood. At some stage after it left Glastonbury, two silver bands were put around the vessel, presumably to strengthen it. This addition apparently caused its healing powers to be lessened.

The type of wood used in its making has led to some doubt as to its age. Some say it was made of a type of oak to be found in Palestine in Christ's time which would verify its authenticity. Maple has been suggested, but also Wych Elm. If the latter is correct, then it casts doubt upon the age of the vessel and gives ammunition to the faction that insists the Nanteos Cup is no more than a mazer—a medieval drinking bowl. In 1952, the Powell family sold their country seat, and the Nanteos Cup went with the property.

If the Grail be a simple wooden dish or an ornate chalice—what does it matter? It may well be that its physical appearance depends solely upon how the individual perceives the Grail to be. The nature of the holy treasure is that it is all things to all men—a universal vision as well as a personal one. Investigating its differences and its universality will be an essential part of our study.

The Hallows

The oft-mentioned Hallows ("holy" or "consecrated") usually refers to the "Four Treasures." In the Irish tradition, the *Tuatha de Danaan* are the Spear of Lugh, the Stone of Fal, the Sword of Light of Nuada, and Dagda's Cauldron. In the Arthurian canon, the Fisher King is the guardian of the four "hallows"—the Sword, which is broken, the Spear of the *Dolorous Blow*, the Dish, and the Grail.

These are to be seen in a modified version as the regalia of the British monarchy, viz., the Sceptre or Rod of Equity and Mercy, the Swords of State, the Ampulla of Holy Oil, and the Crown itself. These treasures are kept in the Tower of London, a place once called the "White Mount" that was sacred many millennia before the advent of any coronation. Ravens have always made their home about the Tower, and it is said that as long as they remain, Britain will never be conquered. The raven is the creature that preserves the soul of Arthur after his death. A country saying that it is ill-luck to kill a raven is probably based upon this tradition.

The Hallows represent the growth of consciousness. They are also the four elements and the four humours—the latter a notion of *physic* given much credence by our ancestors. In order for wisdom to be achieved, the seeker must embrace each of the four virtues (Justice, Prudence, Temperance, and Fortitude) and in doing so, attain a balanced personality. The quaternary, or four-foldness, is a universal symbol, often representing the world.

Royal Blood

In 1982, the controversial work *The Holy Blood and The Holy Grail* was published.[5] It received some interest and much notoriety for its assertions. The authors claimed that Jesus was wed to Mary Magdalene, and that they had several children together. This is now almost an accepted view in mainstream spiritual thinking, but it was not at the time the book appeared. Then, many considered its assertions to be blasphemous. Another perhaps less radical premise was that Christ's descendants were the Merovingian dynasty in Southern France.

The main theme of the book was not original. Donovan Joyce had published *The Jesus Scroll* in 1972 based upon a similar premise. The evidence for his conclusions was contained in a document apparently discovered during archaeological excavations in Israel. The "scroll" had then been stolen and offered to the author who subsequently obtained it. Joyce then maintained that Israeli security forces had taken the scroll from him in Tel Aviv airport. It was said to now be held in the Vatican.

Joyce died in 1980, and *The Holy Blood* text appeared shortly after. One of its co-authors, Michael Baigent, later reiterated the assertion that in the Vatican were documents that proved the thesis proposed in their own book. In the twenty-first century, Dan Brown exploited the same theme with great financial gain to himself. The whole affair has since become part of urban myth.

The Arthuriad follows closely the notion of "Holy Blood," a method the Ancient Egyptians employed to preserve the royal line. Keeping the bloodline "pure" was of paramount concern to the dynastic Pharaohs and was the reason for the then-common practice of incest among royal families. In the Arthurian tradition,

Merlin desired that Arthur would be born of a mother who was part of a magickal hierarchy, as he was himself. He chose Ygerna—High Priestess of Atlantis—for the role. If the king, her offspring, had a magickal pedigree, Merlin believed he would then be able to communicate with the king through the Inner Planes.

The royal bloodline has existed in Britain since the time of Egbert of Wessex in the ninth century. He was *bretwalda,* the first "ruler of Britain." The previous monarch—Elizabeth II—is related to Egbert. She also claims William I "the Conqueror" as an ancestor (a great-grandfather of twenty-nine generations). The tradition of "divine rule" in Britain stems from the longevity of the royal line. Its magickal essence originates in the time of Arthur, the king who defended his subjects with divine aid against the invader.

Graal, Greal, or *Grail* means "dish." *Sangreal, San Grial,* and *Sang Rial* contain a reference to "royal blood" via a pun in Old French. As an object, the "Grail" referred originally to a cruet. This was once in the keeping of Joseph of Arimathea and within it was the blood of Christ. A variation in legend of the Grail being a cup was the citing of two such cruets, the other containing the sweat of Christ.

Developing upon the role of Mary Magdalene as Christ's lover, another tradition is that she actually is the Grail—a Christian variation upon the theme of the Goddess personifying the cauldron. In another interpretation, Valentin Tomberg speaks of the magickal power of the holy blood as being the manifestation of divine and earthly power.

> *"...it is there, and only there, that the power of sacred magic resides. This power is, in the last analysis that of twofold sincerity—divine and human—united in the human word or action. Because not one word or action is truly sincere when it is only cerebral, and when it is only cerebral then it is not a flow of vital blood. The more sincerity there is in the human word or action, the more there is the vital essence of blood. When it happens...the human wish is in accord with the divine."*[6]

The Grail Journey

A text of the fourth century describes Joseph of Arimathea journeying with the Grail to "The White Isle"—Britain. Joseph resided in Glastonbury and founded the first Christian church, later secreting the Grail in the Chalice Well. Just before his death, Joseph requested of God that none might possess the Grail unless they were of his lineage. As his descendants, only the Rich Fisher (or Fisher King) and the knight Sir Perceval were entitled to this legacy.

At this point in history, early in the first century AD, the Grail adopts its metaphysical form and discards its material aspect. The sacred space that the Grail occupied was from that time on inviolate. It could not be touched by chaos, turmoil, or bloodshed. Its intrinsic power, as all magick, was neutral. If the crusaders wished to see the Grail as the sufferings of Christ, they were free to do so; that was only one of the infinite associations assigned to it. It may just as well have been a symbol of Muslim pain as well, and if man desired to use the power of the Grail for his own ends, then so be it. Great evil has often been perpetrated in the name of God. In the twentieth century, every soldier of the *Wermacht*—the German army—had the words *Gott mit uns* ("God is with us") inscribed upon his uniform belt buckle.

Inevitably, the pursuit of some sacred object was to continue. The crusaders had failed to find the Grail in the desert, so where was it? Was it held by the Cathars, hiding in their mountain fortress of Montsegur in the Languedoc area of France? Condemned as heretics by the Church, in 1244, their refuge had been besieged and taken. Those who had remained were burnt at the stake before the gates of the castle. A rumour that a small group had escaped with "the great treasure," gave rise to the rumour that the Cathars still held the Grail. This incident will return in different circumstances later in our account.

The Knights Templar were the next group to be associated with the Holy Vessel. They were intimate with Arabic nobility and may even have acquired The Ark of the Covenant from them. Throughout the fourteenth century, the Templars had the reputation of being the new guardians of the Grail. A fascinating account of the Templar Fleet, the Order's private navy, sailing to Oak Island off Nova Scotia and secreting the Grail there has been posited. The "Money Pit" is the supposed hiding place of the holy vessel, though it must be said that claims for the deep shaft concealing the jewels of Marie Antoinette have also been made.

Whether the Templars possessed the Grail or not, its powers did not subsequently guarantee any protection from ill. They were to be hounded by the Dominican inquisition for supposed "heathen practices," including the "worship" of the Grail. To the Church, their misplaced reverence for Mary Magdalene hastened their condemnation. In 1312, as a result of political machinations by Philip IV of France and Pope Clement, the Order was bloodily disbanded. Many escaped to England where, to the credit of the reigning monarch Edward III, they were left to their own devices.

In the later Middle Ages, the Church might have employed the Grail as a symbol of faith, but they chose not to admit even of its existence. In the minds of the people, it was considered to be a symbol of peace and fulfillment, even ecstasy. The troubadours played a great part in keeping alive the ancient traditions that had centered about the Grail. These merry minstrels preserved in song and fable the inner truths concerning the holy vessel, and for that reason, they greatly deserve our thanks.

The Secret

The marvellous outcome was that the Grail went into hiding, choosing for itself who was to be its guardian. This appointed keeper, as well as being sworn to total secrecy, would also be anonymous. The Grail too would appear as a mundane object, one easily overlooked. Only when it was revered by a devotee would it reveal its true nature. Neither does a magician stand out in the crowd, though he will be recognised by those who have the same vibration. Going about their ordinary business, occultists must conceal their supernatural light most carefully.

With the coming of Christianity to the West came the learning of the monks. An intellectual dimension was added to the Grail. No longer was the idea of the simple cup considered to be enough; layers of meaning had to be attributed to it. These multifarious qualities, some of them quite contradictory, gave the Grail a superficial gloss rather than adding anything to its aura. The key to understanding the Grail is to realise that it is a symbol of universal perfection. This is not a matter of exclusion, for the Grail embraces every atom in the cosmos.

Wisdom is the essence that is derived from knowledge. The sagacity that the Grail teaches has echoes in every spiritual tradition. We would do well to consider the symbol of the lotus, as it has much in common with the Grail. This sacred flower is nature's way of bringing together the abstract and the concrete universe. The lotus neatly represents the four elements and is a supreme example of the quaternary. Its roots are in the Earth below, passing through Water, and flowering in the Air, its growth brought about by the Fire of the Sun. The progress of the soul from darkness to light is embodied by its seeds falling into the Water. These will eventually continue the eternal cycle of life.

The bloom was sacred in Ancient Egypt, India, and Tibet. It later became the lily held by the Archangel Gabriel. The dominion of this heavenly messenger is the West—and the element associated with it—Water. The shape of the flower is a spray, signifying the Fire element. Fire complements Water to produce creation and generation. White and red are significant colours of this polarity—purity and energy combined.

Gabriel is the angel who bears the message of the Annunciation to the Virgin Mary. In the same way the Bodhisattva reveals to Maha-Maya, the mother of Gautama, that the Buddha will also be a Saviour of the world. Isis and Osiris are represented by the lotus-flower as the "fires of intelligence." The sacred word—as exemplified by the teachings of Christ—is symbolised by "tongues of fire."

Vision of Perfection

Valentin Tomberg was one of the great visionaries of the twentieth century. His exhaustive study of the Major Arcana of the Tarot is one of the most impressive works upon the subject. That his words are applicable in a wider context than the Tarot is demonstrated in this text.

"...goodness, truth, and beauty do not lose their attraction from century to century; that, in spite of all, there is faith, hope, and charity in the world; that there are saints, sages, geniuses, benefactors, and

healers; that pure thought, poetry, music, and prayer are not being engulfed in the void; that there is this universal miracle of human history; and that the miraculous exists."[7]

Spiritual writings are to be found all over the world. The "Grail Literature" is one of a litany of texts. However, it is apparent that writings about the Grail far exceed those concerned with any other treasure. Here may be one of its many attributes—it inspires the artist as did the Cauldron of Cerridwen prompt the bards to compose their verses. References to the Grail occur often within Western poetry and philosophy.

Whatever the Grail might be—artefact, vision, or idea—it relies on being perceived by man for its actual existence. It may well have been present in the universe in some form millions upon millions of years before the advent of *homo sapiens*. Consider the Grail as something that reflects the essence of those who lived in a particular era. Times change and we change with them, so our notion of the Grail alters constantly.

The Grail is a microcosm of the universe, and so completely at one with it that its form is indistinguishable from our own consciousness. More than an actual object existing in a specific time and place, the Grail is a metaphysical occurrence. Christ taught that "unless a man be born again, he cannot see the kingdom of God." This is echoed in Egyptian tradition with the story of Osiris. The "death" of Osiris is simply his re-birth on a higher plane—the "Baptism of the Mind" to the Egyptians. The personal surrenders to the universal—the initiate becomes "the Cup Bearer of God." Immortal, deathless in Spirit, all is gained by being in the presence of the Grail.

In the Egyptian pantheon of gods, Horus, the son of Osiris, does not reflect the saviour, but the exemplar. His role is to reveal the way to immortality. The credo of Horus is that one must strive to achieve growth within the soul. It is akin to a Protestant work ethic combined with a realization of karma! "What ye sow, so shall ye reap." Those who fail will be judged sternly by Horus. Their master will inscribe upon their school report— "not enough diligence."

Horus was the protector of Ra and the champion of the gods. He fought the evil Set who had murdered his father. The rank of Horus is of the highest, for he holds the sceptre of power. Ra, "the King of Duration" and "Master in Eternity" could only be approached through him. His wand is powerless unless it is used in combination with a conscience. That quality is owned by Maat, the goddess of Justice and Judgment. The Ancient Egyptians would actively demonstrate their obedience to Ra by refraining from doing evil. They believed that upon following the Laws of Maat, it was ensured that the individual had control over his own destiny. The Knights of the Round Table as protectors of the truth are, like Horus, a symbol of all that is noble.

Arthur may have been the last hero in the West who knew the old gods. A supernatural being himself, he intuitively established a rapport with those ancient forces. Arthur has much in common with Horus—they are both war-like and a protector of all things sacred. Both represent the Sun at noon when it is at its most powerful. They are, respectively, the lion and the hawk-headed man. Horus is also spoken of as the World Saviour and the Shining Light. The Eye of Horus, the *Wadjet*, is a powerful symbol of protection. It is also the Eye of Mind and reflects the illumination that is central to the Egyptian tradition. Hathor, sometimes the wife, at other times the parent of Horus, is known as the "Mother of Light."

The nature of the Grail is holotropic—a state that embraces the totality of existence. When we mediate, we should begin with no actual conception of the Grail, then let it grow organically from the seeds of its own illumination. It is said that the Grail represents all life in a single, golden drop. It is limitless light and, by definition, will contain the greatest darkness within it. Teilhard de Chardin described the noosphere as:

> "...the living membrane which is stretched like a film over the lustrous surface of the star which holds us. An ultimate envelope taking on its own individuality and gradually detaching itself like a luminous aura...the Very Soul of the Earth."[8]

He spoke of the aura that was common to us all and remarked that:

"Nothing is precious except that part of you which is in other people and that part of others which is in you. Up there, on high, everything is one."[9]

This reflective quality gives to the Grail its limitless and eternal power. The Grail, in its ability to change, is like Mercurius. A cosmic being, capable of incarnating into any form from an eagle to a sunbeam, he is:

"...the spirit...which fills the whole world and in the beginning swam upon the waters...the spirit of Truth, which is hidden from the world."[10]

The Grail is a symbol implanted deep in the collective unconscious. Because the Grail is hidden, it is somehow regarded by the dull as suspect—subversive. The subtle, as the occult, runs counter to much modern thinking. Our society has an endless hunger for access to every gobbet of information. We are not permitted to have secrets—the State and the media does not approve. Thus, the Grail is transformed once more—it becomes a symbol of eccentricity, even rebellion.

II. GOD AND GODDESS

"WE CAN...SEEK HARMONY AND BALANCE BY
REUNITING THE FEMININE AND MASCULINE
ASPECTS OF OURSELVES. WE MAY THEN WALK
THIS WORLD WITH COMPASSION, COURAGE,
AND WISDOM. "

— LINDSEY PATON

In every era, both male and female archetypes are redefined. One wonders if in the coming centuries, the male species might gradually become redundant. Will the gender balance be weighed unalterably towards the distaff side? Consider—by means of *invitro* fertilization, a woman may conceive a child independent of any man. In the West, a same-sex relationship is generally regarded as acceptable. The "gay scene," far from being the clandestine and furtive practice it once was, is now part of mainstream society.

Certain images fall into disfavour while new templates are constantly created. To illustrate this, one may cite the culture of the 1960s when, with the advent of the Beatles and other pop groups, it became fashionable for young men to wear their hair long. Those who did sport these lengthy locks were often the object of vilification and often overt hostility. Despite the historical precedent of Celtic warriors, cavaliers, and pioneers of the Old West, this "look" was unacceptable to the majority. Post-war thinking still adhered to a military ideal—an unalterable image of how a "man" should look.

Of archetypes, Jung proposed that there were a distinct group, among them: the Child, Great Mother, Sage, Trickster, Devil, Scarecrow, and Mentor. Jung suggested that our "knowing" of archetypal images was not racially inherited. A motif may be the same in a different culture. One of the most potent archetypes—the hero—may be known in exactly the same detail to those who are continents apart.

Jung's thesis is that our unconscious self creates these images. He insists that they have, like myths, a valuable role to play in keeping an equilibrium within our inner being. Without this element in our lives we feel bereft, as if a profound part of our individual self is absent. Swiss Jungian psychologist Marie Louis von Franz emphasized that an archetypal image *"touches the heart just as much as the mind."* She explained that,

> *"Archetypal dream images and the images of the great myths and religions still have about them a little of the 'cloudy' nature of absolute knowledge in that they always seem to contain more than we can assimilate consciously, even by means of elaborate interpretations. They always retain an ineffable and mysterious quality that seems to reveal to us more than we can really know."*[11]

Is it possible that we actually manifest these images, in particular, the heroic? The saying "cometh the hour, cometh the man" seems most pertinent with reference to the history of Britain. Great leaders have emerged in times when our kingdom was in danger. The word "hero" literally means "protector" or "defender." It is a symbol of the ego, the individual.

When watching a drama, the audience particularly identifies with such a figure, living his trials, triumphs, and eventual fate in surrogate fashion. The post-modernist "anti-hero," although he may possess radically different virtues to his conventional counterpart, still arouses sympathy and a strong emotional response. Thus, he is still in the archetypal hero mould but tailored to the modern era.

Gods and Kings

We might suggest that by being consistently empowered, the "classic" heroic archetypes in the "collective unconscious" gain a super-reality. The image of King Arthur, known to the world for nearly a thousand years, still stimulates the collective psyche. Encountering these denizens of the inner world stimulates a response in the soul as well as the mind. It is significant that archetypal images, although always potent, are always encountered as an impression, something not visually precise.

In Western myth, King Arthur represents the zenith of male power—the Divine King. In correspondence with the Tarot, he is, in worldly terms, the card of *The Emperor*. In the divine realm, he is represented by the card of *The Sun*. Various solar gods are related to him as we shall see.

The tragedy of Arthur as *The Emperor* is that he does not desire *The Empress*—the fair Guinevere. Arthur yearns to be reunited with his feminine self, the *anima*, but this union, when it occurs, will be with another Arcanum of the Tarot—*Death*—his Scorpionic love, Morgan le Fay. She is the crone figure within the Moon. In her, Arthur finds his own personal Grail, but at a great cost to himself and the kingdom.

Images within the Tarot are helpful to our study. The archetypes that are depicted in the Major Arcana come from many different cultures. *The Emperor* is Teutonic, *The Hierophant* has his origins in the Russian Orthodox Church, *The Wheel of Fortune* stems from India, and *Death* probably refers to the medieval plagues.

In 1778, Antoine Court de Gébelin referred to the *tarraux* as a *"game of Egyptian origin."* Its etymology, like everything else about it, is diverse. The name may be composed of two Oriental words *tar* and *rha* or *rho* meaning "Royal Road." Other suggestions are that the name derives from the Sanskrit *taru* meaning "deck of cards" or *Torah*, the Hebraic "Law." Whatever its origins, the Tarot, perhaps more than any other mystical tradition, is rich in symbolism.

The images of the Ryder/Waite Tarot are familiar enough not to need an extensive explanation of their appearance. The changing context of the Tarot is, however, relevant to our journey, one that follows the path of Sun God and Moon Maiden. It is significant that Isis, who holds almost a monopoly amongst goddesses in the Egyptian pantheon, features so strongly in the Tarot. In the old packs, she was *The Papess,* but has been restored to her more fitting title of *The High Priestess.*

The inner life of Britain is reflected in its folk tales and place names. It is this undercurrent of spiritual strength that gives the landscape its beauty and majesty and, in the same way, Arthur his power. The land is literally the rock upon which the British stand. For the visitor to Britain, all may merely become a swirling, superficial tide of impressions—a reflection of the culture at any given time. Yet, true Britain resides in the heart and soul of the kingdom.

For those with republican sympathies, the image of Arthur as a king in majesty might seem to be unpalatable. It is true that much has changed in England since the Industrial Revolution. The popular voice reflects the spiritual well-being of the nation, and the English spirit has edged more toward the rebel than the monarch.

The pirate and the vagabond—Robin Hood, Bonnie Prince Charlie, and Rob Roy—have suddenly become more appealing. Yet, this anarchic stance may have tipped the balance too far. Since the end of the twentieth century, an attitude of defiance has become the norm. Youth, naturally non-conformist, has been whipped into an artificial frenzy by an insidious media. Showing outward respect to any authority figure is no longer cool or fashionable. Some of the liberal elite even propose that there should be no visible hallmark of rank in society at all. How times have changed!

Yet, the icon remains intact and will always do so. Arthur rules by "divine right" because he has sworn to serve the kingdom. His power is thus bestowed on him by Heaven. The root of the word "kingdom" is *kin*, meaning ancestry. This is the "royal blood," the pure lineage that links those who rule. The king willingly "sheds his blood" for his people and, in ancient tradition, this meant the sacrifice of the old leader to usher in the new. "The King is dead, long live the King" is the telling announcement made to the people in Britain at the passing of their monarch. The implication is that the kingdom is never left for one moment without a guardian.

There have been good kings and bad kings and there always will be. It is the way of the world to judge, often in an arbitrary fashion. The people may praise a benign monarch, but when they are threatened, they cheer all the louder for the warrior hero who has defended them. It is he who is remembered in history, not his liberal counterpart—hence the image of a king as a martial figure. Study the Tarot card of *The Emperor*—beneath his cloak he wears his armour and is always ready to take up arms, hopefully for right.

Fisher King

Pelles, the Fisher King, is the keeper of the *Grail Hallows* and, by definition, guardian of the Grail. Arthur is king of the outer world, but Pelles rules the inner kingdom. The curse that is upon the Waste Land, the suffering that it endures is personified in the Fisher King. In the Arthurian Tales, the Fisher King (French: *pecheur*—sinner, fisherman) represents sacrifice and worse still—impotence.

The Fisher King may too be an allegory of the seasonal round. In winter, the seed lays cold and dormant waiting for the warmth of spring. The Fisher King is in a state of limbo, waiting for the Grail to restore life to the Waste Land. His state of infertility is disastrous to his role as guardian of the kingdom. The king's spirit is reflected in the state of the kingdom—lassitude spells ruin. The space that the Fisher King occupies is one of a surreal limbo. He may have endured this state for all eternity or merely a moment. In the Waste Land, time stands still.

It is Perceval's naivety in not asking the Grail Question, *"Whom does the Grail Serve?"* that ensures the Waste Land will not be restored to wholeness.[12] Sir Balin wounds the Grail King with one of the Hallows—the Spear of Destiny. The wound the Fisher King receives—known as the dolorous stroke—further condemns Pelles and the kingdom to its fate. With this rash act, all is now profaned; the Grail Castle falls into ruin and the Grail Hallows disappear. The demise of the Fisher King may be a symbol of the end of the Age of Pisces. This period of two millennia, personified by Christ, is also symbolised by the Grail.

But the Fisher King, though he may have fallen further into darkness and despair, may be returned to the light—like Osiris. In the Egyptian pantheon, this god is referred to as "The Lord of Fish." Osiris is the vegetation god who is destroyed and restored, as every year the crops return once more in the Nile Valley. His sacrifice is nothing if not total as he is dismembered by his enemy, Set. With the aid of Thoth, the god of magick and healing, his consort Isis makes his body whole again.[13] In this resurrection, the ancient Egyptians made much of the spiritual journey after death—a journey they considered to be one that went from darkness into light.

A hope that the land will be restored is promised by the nature of the Fisher King's wound. His blood falls to the Earth and will eventually be transformed into Fire (the Sun) and Water (rain). Together, these elements will eventually restore fertility to the sterile kingdom. Galahad heals the Fisher King and the land when he eventually gains the Grail. The Fisher King may be the shadow of King Arthur before the Grail is restored. He too will be made whole again when he is reunited with his inner self in the kingdom of Avalon, though he must wait for death to gain a state of peace

Tides of the Moon

Since ancient times, the feminine principle has been symbolized by the Moon. She has no light of her own and relies upon the Sun for illumination. Because of this, the lunar body has been regarded as somehow inferior to the solar. This is an erroneous view, for:

> *"Without the Moon there would be no moonbeams, no month, no lunacy, no Apollo program, less poetry, and a world where every night was dark and gloomy."[14]*

To expand our understanding, it is possible that we may reverse this thesis and regard the Moon as being an "external" entity. Is it that the Moon looks outward from itself and finds inspiration in the doings of others? The Moon rules the tides and the cycles that govern fertility, both in the land and the female body. Traditionally, the two elements of Earth and Water are regarded as feminine. Earth has the power to contain Water so it is stored and not dissipated, though it must at intervals be permitted to flow. Water is essential to existence and no life can survive without it. The element of Water is by nature flowing, weaving, and free. It reflects, and thus divines, the hidden meaning of all that occurs. Water, like humanity, has its moods—from cruel to calm. The Goddess knows that no act is ever exclusively good or bad. One merely balances the other so that the universe continues to maintain equilibrium.

Wells have a strong emotional quality. We speak of "a well of loneliness," one of silence, joy, youth, and immortality. There have been "healing" wells since ancient times. Our ancestors knew that the beneficial powers of a well are most potent at certain times and seasons. Beltane and Midsummer's Eve were regarded as auspicious occasions for healing. Norse mythology has Mimir's Well, the Greeks—the Fountain of Parnassus, and Judaism—the Well of The Seven. In the Isle of Avalon is the Chalice Well, where the Grail may still lie hidden. In Avalon, it is said that "the veil is thin." The sight of the Grail is perhaps akin to the Moon with her fitful and unpredictable appearances, perhaps explaining the delight we feel with these images.

The well and the fish are symbols of the Goddess. The *Vesica Piscis*, adopted as a Christian symbol, may be an ancient depiction of the goddess form. As the Goddess in one of her many forms is a healer, the custom of tying votive offerings to a tree near the well has its own logical purpose. As these pieces of coloured cloth gradually rotted, so the illness or misfortune of the supplicant passed away. The legacy of this tradition is the throwing of coins into a "wishing well."

The "holy well" is considered to be an entrance to the Other World. The word "holy" originates from *Hel*, goddess of the Underworld. This entrance is guarded by a powerful spirit. The least alarming might be a cat, bird, or fish. If it has a human form, it might be a hideous hag or a beautiful maiden, both a personification of the Moon. Every well is protected by the Great Serpent, which winds its coils about the entrance. Ishtar is the ruler of springs, and from them, this goddess raises serpent energy.

The Serpent

The protective focus of the Serpent extends beyond wells to other sacred sites. When the Buddha spent seven days beneath the Bhodi tree, the Serpent King *Mucalinda* wrapped seven coils about the prophet so his meditation would not be interrupted. Snakes always defend their ground and do not retreat, hence their superiority as a guardian.

This cold-blooded vertebrate might appear alien to humanity, yet it is linked within our own physical self. In Eastern teachings, energy generated in the medulla and traveling along the spinal cord is referred to as the *kundalini*. It may be aroused or "raised" so that the subtle energies rise through the body and bring about a state of enlightenment. Hence, the association of the snake with wisdom *"be ye as wise as serpents and as gentle as doves,"* as the Bible has it. The serpent is also seen as a divine creature with the power to affect the outcome of human affairs. It has a paradoxical nature in its power to inflict death or to heal, and thus, restore life.

The *Caduceus*, two entwined serpents, is the token of Hermes— the messenger of the gods. It is the international symbol of medicine and denotes Hermes' other role as a healer. In Hindu mythology, Vishnu floats upon the cosmic waters on the serpent *Shesha*. *Quetzalcoatl* is the great serpent who embodies the sky in the Mayan tradition. The *basilisk*, the serpent god of the Phoenicians, and the Norse *Midgard* serpent have the same role.

The Serpent was the infamous resident of the Garden of Eden, tempting Eve to eat of the Tree of Knowledge—an act expressly forbidden by God. The Bible is not clear about the serpent's motives, one view being that the serpent's beauty, and more significantly, its wisdom, caused the creature to succumb to its own pride. The serpent entered an intellectual dispute with God as to the nature of Truth and presumably lost the argument. He then willfully bestowed knowledge upon Man as an act of revenge. The words of Papus, the *nom de plume* of occultist Gerard Encausse, are relevant here:

> *"Each man, a reflected molecule of humanity made in its image contains in himself an Adam, the source of the Will—this is the Brain; an Eve, source of the intelligence—the heart; and he should balance the heart by the brain, and the brain by the heart, to become a centre of divine love."*[15]

As the first recipient of that knowledge, woman was roundly condemned for the next two millennia as being the bringer of ill fortune to man. In medieval illustrations, the serpent is often depicted in a female form, thus emphasizing this ridiculous judgment.

The Hebrew word for "serpent" comes from the root *nachsach*, meaning to practise divination and to observe signs and omens. The Church has an antipathy to all forms of divination, believing that God's purpose should be the only acceptable outcome of destiny. Perhaps the serpent's insights were seen as a substantial threat to the doctrine later promulgated by established religion.

Alchemy and Polarity

The essential principle of alchemy is that the human spirit (symbolized as gold) is tried and tested by the fire heating the crucible (representing life). The tenets of alchemical practice include *the unum vas* ("one vessel"), the *una medicina*, and the *unus lapis*. This association with the female and her desire for union with the male principle has its practical exposition in the chemical action of red sulphur being mingled with white. The alchemists regarded this as a meeting of "gold" with "silver." The female nature must blend completely with the male—the Great Mother absorbing the masculine into her womb. This coming together, enacted in the otherworld, manifests as *lapis lazuli*. This is the substance of the philosopher's stone or *Rosarium Philosophorium*. The word *Gar-al* means "the cup of stone." This may be a reference to the emerald that reportedly fell from Lucifer's forehead when he was cast out of heaven by his fellow angels.

There is a world of difference between polarity and duality. The latter concept has caused untold harm to the expansion of the mental processes and to the psychic health of millions throughout the ages. A lazy substitute for incisive thought, dreary old duality is the deadweight of fundamentalism in religion. As Heraclitus declared, *"To God, all things are fair and good and right, but men hold some things wrong and some right."* [16]

The belief that the opposite of an accepted notion can only be incorrect, even reprehensible, is anathema to any debate or even any sensible perception of the world. "Comparisons are odious" as Nanny used to say! Notions of good and evil, black and white, even male and female should be put aside. Heaven and Hell are inventions of man, not the cosmos. Resign the idea to the mental scrapheap where it belongs!

The greatest proponent of this intellectual fallacy has been the Christian Church. A ruling elite from 1100 AD onwards, it owned the power to decide what was ultimately "good" or "evil" and persecuting those it condemned. Having the authority via its armies and through its courts, it brought torture and death to countless "heretics"—innocent men and women.

If we wish to play the Christians at their own game, we have only to present them with a simple proposition. God created the world—there is good and evil existing in the world—therefore God is both good and evil. The equation has more theological backbone than much of the Christian ethic. The premise is not one that leads automatically to atheism, often the refuge of the intellectual.

The temple of faith is built upon accepting that what occurs is supposed to occur. The way this is achieved will not necessarily always be to the individual's liking, but that is almost irrelevant. Those, like the knights upon their Quest who choose to walk upon the path of enlightenment, must pass through a period of darkness as well as that of light. It is their faith that will sustain them.

The magician unerringly follows the principle that "divine will" exists—his power will only operate successfully if it is in harmony with Heaven. He also knows that the spirit of the Temple resides with the High Priestess—its guardian and its keeper. By combining their power in an equal exchange, the spark is created for a magickal working. In any relationship, this can be considered one of the keys to harmony, for it advocates the *blending* of the sexes, not a confrontation between the two. Dion Fortune speaks of *"The begettings and matings of the gods and goddesses, by no means always in holy wedlock..."* and, as always, she has a point. [17]

The polarity of priest and priestess is symbolized respectively in Arthur and the Grail. More prosaically, the relationship between the Sun and Moon promotes this notion. The Sun emerges as constant, masculine—the Original Source of Mind and the Spirit from which all life emanates. The Moon is seen as a reflection of Mother Earth and the changeability of an internal nature.

According to the Chinese *Dao*, this intrinsic polarity fuels the workings of the universe. Yang is created by movement, and when this activity reaches its limit, all becomes still—the state of Yin. Tranquility exists until there is a return to movement once more. Within activity there resides the potential of stillness, albeit at the end of a particular cycle, and it follows that stillness has within it the quality of movement. The individual power is the source of the other, producing and reproducing energy in an endless process. Both belong to each other and exist in harmony.

The word "Moon" (Latin, *mensis—month)* indicates that this body was used by the ancients as a measure of time. The earliest calendars are calculated from the passage of the Moon and not the Sun. The Egyptians first conceived the idea of the seasons, each one lasting a period of three months.

The Sun is seen in certain traditions as being a symbol of the soul. Perhaps the correspondence between the heart and the Sun, with Leo ruling that part of the body, accounts for this. The soul lies hidden within us and represents a point of stillness, a place where we are centered. The true self is content with its individuality, fulfilled in its purpose. In this sense it is complete, uninterested in influencing or even interacting with anything beyond itself. This contradicts the usual view of the solar energy, as manifest in Leo, always desiring to attract attention!

Reason and Intuition

In an enlightened age, the female consciousness will not only be acknowledged but awarded an equal status with the male. Regrettably, in our own times, this state of affairs does not exist in many cultures. For too long:

> *"...the care and tendance of the life-giving springs, which lie in the depths of nature have been disregarded. For these sources of spiritual or psychological energy can only be reached, or so the myths and ancient religions say, through a right approach to the feminine essence..."[18]*

Much has been posited concerning the "left and right" hemispheres of the brain. It is considered that the "right brain" is intuitive, while the "left brain" is the sphere of reasoning. With the advance of science, "rational thinking" was assumed to exclusively own a "correct" interpretation of information. Right brain thinking was seen as unreliable, emotional, and above all, associated with the vagaries of womanhood. Research throws an interesting light upon this. It is the function of the right brain to survey and channel incoming information so, by definition, it has a better idea of what is going on in the world than the left brain!

Why did a division of the brain occur in the first place? Probably because the ability to understand was fundamentally very different to the task of precise detailing. The intellect is a self-answering mechanism and prefers theory/quantity over experience/quality. Intuition involves a willingness to employ different modes of thought other than the purely analytical—it is concerned with the inner being of any object or situation. Grasping the ineffable, unique qualities of anything is the goal of the intuitive. By expanding perception so that every shade of meaning is engaged, one nears the absolute. It can be seen that a heterogeneous whole is the outcome—everything impinges on everything else. Its method is opposite to the left brain which continually seeks to compartmentalize all that it encounters.

Revering The Goddess

The Gnostic Trinity, which is the true legacy of Christ's teachings, existed as a doctrine in the first centuries after his departure. This has a distinct difference from the later versions of the Trinity proposed by the Catholic and Protestant Church. The Gnostic version depicts God, the Messiah, and Fortuna. The former is the female personification of wisdom. The Catholic Church replaced Fortuna with the Virgin Mary, and after the Reformation, the Protestant Church put the "Holy Ghost" in her place.

The Medieval Code of Chivalry recognised the intrinsic purity of the Grail. The Christian faith associated this quality with the Virgin Mary, thus was the association with the Grail born. Arthur's conversion from Pagan Celt to Christian occurs at Brides Mound on the Isle of Avalon. This sacred site has strong Pagan and Christian associations. Here, Arthur was believed to have received a crystal cross from the Virgin Mary. The king then alters the device on his shield from the Red Dragon of Celtic origin to a white cross on a green ground—the talisman of the heart and healing. It is said, in some accounts, that he goes into battle with a banner proclaiming the same symbol and thus is given total victory over his enemies.

This revering of the feminine, even in the figure of the Virgin Mary, did not always find favour in the Middle Ages. The medieval attitude towards women was far from enlightened. They were in the unenviable position of expected subservience to their menfolk and impossibly chaste. The notion that a feminine view of the world was even to be considered, let alone taken seriously, would have been anathema in such a world, one dominated by male authority.

Such a view would have been regarded with the greatest suspicion—perverse, if not blatantly subversive. Perhaps this is why the Knights of the Round Table display a rather ambivalent attitude to women. Sir Perceval is said to be, like Arthur, in pursuit of his anima, while the other knights seem obsessed by a virginal ideal manifesting as an ever-unconsummated love. Chastity is a fundamental element in the code of chivalry, and this colours many of the knights' noble escapades. Denial may be simply another indulgence—and a perverse one at that.

As a result, the tone of the Arthurian tales is often misogynistic. The robust, earthy sexuality of the Goddess and the Cauldron is expunged forever by the new faith. The old ways are suppressed and the *Holy* Grail, as it becomes, is assigned an entirely different ethos. The new religion prompts the knights to display an unreal attitude toward the fair maidens that, almost to the point of tedium, they rescue.

Their aseptic attitude also ensures that the female sex gets a uniformly bad press in the later Grail romances. Unless a woman is chaste, virginal, and unapproachable, she is presumed to be indulging in all manner of sin. Morgan le Fay is depicted as an evil sorceress, Guinevere as an adulteress, Elaine the Grail Maiden is a lustful schemer, and Nimue, the Lady of the Lake, a heartless seductress. Minor characters like Elaine or Gwendolyn receive no better treatment.

In the esoteric world where cultural norms do not figure, it is all much simpler. On the Inner Planes, gender roles are reversed, with the male displaying characteristics associated with the feminine and vice versa. At one extreme, the male-dominated female would be the proud, ruthless, and all-powerful sorceress, personified in Morgan le Fay. The sensitive Fisher King represents the other end of this re-ordered sexual spectrum.

III. SUN GOD

"ARTHUR THEN STANDS FOR THE SUN, THE GIVER
OF LIFE, THE RULER OF THE WORLD."

— CHRISTINE HARTLEY

In the *Vedas*, the oldest Hindu scriptures, the Sun and the Moon are lyrically described. Depicted as miraculous vessels, they are eternally hidden in the mountains of heaven. In the Egyptian pantheon, Horus is the god of the sky—one eye the Sun, the other the Moon. The offspring of Isis and Osiris, he is the protector of Ra. The "Eye of Horus," a celebrated motif, is one of the most powerful symbols of protection ever devised. Thus, we begin to gain some understanding of the degree of respect accorded to the most potent of the heavenly bodies.

Our Sun is not the true "mother of the Earth." That honour belongs to an unnamed collection of stars that existed some four and a half billion years ago. Such a cosmic breath of life was extinguished in a supernova, but before dying, it gave the universe the necessary particles of life that make up our physical selves. As Joni Mitchell once sang, *"we are stardust"*—and she was absolutely right.

Having mentioned the physics—what of the myth? People have been worshipping the Sun for many millennia and this great, golden orb still has an unaccountable influence over both our outer and inner lives. It is necessary for our existence, and without its presence, there would be no life in the solar system. It is small wonder that the Sun represents divine power and has also, since ancient times, been adopted as a symbol of earthly dominion. In Egypt, the pharaohs were blessed and were thought to become as Ra, the Sun god. In the Western tradition, the Sun is a symbol of kingship both outwardly and within.

The two great entwined myths of the Western world are those of King Arthur and the Holy Grail. In academia, the medievalist holds sway regarding the Arthuriad. The school displays little patience with a transcendental approach to the *oeuvre*, simply ignoring that essential aspect or dismissing it out of hand. Equally damning are the views of historians in recent years. Many of these pedagogues have vociferously denied that anyone called Arthur even existed in the sixth century.

It might be concluded that, in this case, folk opinion is better informed than the experts. How could King Arthur remain in the consciousness of a nation for a thousand years without having some deep resonance in the psyche of Britain? The acclaim that the Arthurian saga is given throughout the world would seem to prove that Camelot still stands tall in the universal imagination.

Neuroscience is on the side of the mythmaker. Beliefs are firmly entrenched in the intuitive part of our nature. Research has shown that we invariably defend our insights even when they are invaded by reason. When confronted with a "logical argument," we stubbornly stick to those things that make up our faith. Kant spoke of the "transcendental unity of apperception," a concept fundamental to the way that we process information. Comprehension and sensibility are synthesized by understanding. We embrace those things that seem meaningful to us without considering whether they "make sense."

Ignoring the brickbats hurled by the medievalists, we shall strive to establish the "historical" King Arthur. This figure appears in the fifth century AD at the time that the Roman army quit Britain. Rome was besieged by the Goths and Visigoths and its empire was crumbling. In these difficult, almost hopeless, circumstances, one Artorius, or Arthur, a Romano-Celt emerged. He replaced the ruling Ambrosius as the supreme commander of the British people. Arthur held the title of dux bellorum and valiantly fought the Anglo-Saxons from 530 AD onward, winning several major battles in the process. Inevitably, British resistance ended with the fall of Arthur. By the middle of the ninth century, the Saxons had conquered Britain almost entirely.

As a historical figure, Arthur is then largely forgotten. In the thirteenth century, French writers searching for a hero for their romances came upon him. Arthur was rediscovered and given a cast of characters to surround him—a queen, a wizard as a mentor, and a court adorned with noble knights.

Much has been made of the supposed gap between the historical and the mythical Arthur. Tom Shippey, who wrote extensively on the arch myth-maker Tolkien, suggested that *"myth resolves contradictions."* Perhaps more tellingly, Hans Leisegang explains that:

> *"Every myth expresses, in a form narrated for a particular case, an eternal idea, which will be intuitively recognised by he who re-experiences the content of the myth."*[19]

If there is an absence of written or pictorial records about any historical figure, then any account of them will fall back on what is no more than hearsay. Some folk tales seem to grow more magnificent with the telling. Who are we to say that in them is not a kernel of truth?

It may be that titles such as "Arthur" and "Merlin" were initiatic. An elevated status was attached to certain individuals and their title was synonymous with their virtues. This is borne out by a reference to one Celtic leader as being "no Arthur." It seems that standards in Celtic Britain were always high.

Like the ancient religions that honour an animal or plant as the ancestor of their race, the hero must be seen as a human manifestation of the divine. The template for heroic tales was established in the classical era, if not before—the hero is always fatherless yet descended from a superhuman. Arthur qualifies on both counts, having Uther Pendragon impregnate his mother Ygerna by way of Merlin's sorcery. The legends speak of Ygerna as having been a priestess in Atlantis who, like Merlin, escaped the destruction of the sacred island. Thus are Arthur's magickal antecedents established.

Excalibur

The Arthuriad abounds in symbolism and each stage of Arthur's life is represented by a potent image. These are the Sword in the Stone, the Crown, Excalibur, The Round Table, and Camelot. The most powerful of all appears at the end of the saga—the Holy Grail. Let us first examine the sword, a valuable possession—one that bestowed high status upon its owner—and a deadly weapon. In these times, the swordsmiths of England were held in high regard by the rest of the world.

The sword represents the sharp and often deadly blow—the quick response. Away from the more obvious associations of combat, it speaks of the honed edge of incisive thinking. Decisions are made swiftly and with confidence. It is essential for the warrior, as it is for the king, to own this quality.

Freeing the blade from its earthly confines was achieved in the celebrated act of pulling the sword from the stone. Such a scene demonstrated that the divine powers were in accord with Arthur. Heaven released the sword of power into the care of its appointed keeper. A sword being held aloft, as Arthur must have done as soon as he drew it from the stone, is a gesture of triumph and victory. In the *Ace of Swords* of the Tarot, the blade is surmounted by a crown and laurel leaves. Victory reflects great glory upon the individual and those who follow him. The sword also represents justice of a worldly nature—a dispute that must be resolved. Not necessarily a physical combat, a war of words could be fought, but the combatants are still just as in earnest.

Excalibur features in the episode of the Lady of the Lake and is assigned much greater powers than the Sword in the Stone. It is the scabbard, however, that has even more power—of a more subtle quality—than the sword itself. The scabbard boasts the power to heal any wound sustained in battle. On another level, the association of the scabbard being the female recipient of the thrusting sword is almost too obvious to be dwelt upon. Sexual union is often at the heart of much that occurs in myth.

It was said that in battle, the light from Excalibur blinded the enemies of Arthur, and this happened because they did not possess his higher nature. His inner light was not only manifest on the battlefield; it was the illumination that he needed to guide him upon his spiritual path.

After their brief tryst, Morgan le Fay dedicates much of her energy to harassing Arthur. In an attempt to steal Excalibur, she enters the king's bed chamber only to discover Arthur asleep with the sword firmly in his grip. Not wishing to risk his wrath if she were to be discovered, the sorceress is content to make off with the scabbard. Arthur wakes, sees what has happened, and sets off in pursuit of the thief. Morgan le Fay outwits her pursuers by changing herself into a rock, but not before hurling the scabbard into the Lake.

Arthur's fortunes take a dramatic turn for the worse after this episode. The kingdom is thrust into civil war because of Guinevere's infidelity and Arthur stands helpless as the knight fights his brother. His own end comes when he is fatally wounded by Mordred, his own son by Morgan, in the final battle.

Excalibur has "take me" in runic script on one side of the blade and "cast me away" on the other. When Arthur's sacred task has been fulfilled, the timeless weapon must be returned from whence it came. There is a Celtic tradition of making offerings of weapons to the river god *Silvanus*. This may have been the origin of the tale of casting Excalibur into the Lake.

The Grail Sword, one of the Grail Hallows, has an obscure lineage. Apparently being the sword of David the King, it was placed in a mysterious ship by Solomon to sail the seas until it was discovered. Supposedly, it could only be received by Sir Galahad, confirming his abject purity.

In another strand of the tale, the sword broke when it was used to force entrance into an earthly paradise. We may surmise this represents the notion that it is unwise to employ spiritual things to gain the material world. Another version states that it was the duty of Gawain and Perceval to take the sword to the forge of Wayland, the legendary sword maker, and there it would be restored to its original state. It is often, like Excalibur, referred to as the "Sword of Light."

Sun God

Arthur the warrior king is transformed into a man of myth—the Sun God—and in this role he follows Mithras and Adonis, figures of classical mythology. Arthur is first the *wunderkind*, then the leader who gathers a holy assembly as his court, and finally, the god/king who sacrifices himself in battle. That he will return and be resurrected is an established part of the tale.

Sacred words are part of the myth of Apollo, the Sun god, as are music and songs of praise. Thoth, the Egyptian god of magick is the "voice of Ra," the command of creation. In the Egyptian tradition, Ra is regarded not only as the god of the Sun, but the ineffable power that created the Sun and the universe. The opening line of the Gospel of St. John echoes this sentiment—*"In the beginning was the Word."*

Another quotation from the same gospel concerns the words of Christ, *"I am the Light of the World."* The light of illumination should enhance the ideas that we have gleaned from our observations and our experience. Such a light should not be fitful, "a flash in the pan," or it achieves nothing. We must also not lose the quality of innocence that we possess when we enter the world. As the poet Tennyson says of the child, he comes "trailing clouds of glory," meaning that traces of heaven, and thus the divine truth, are still about him at birth.

Was Christ an adaption of an already existing deity? Clearly, The Church deliberately usurped the festival of Mithras on December twenty-fifth and replaced it with *Christ*mas Day. Sir James Frazer, the Victorian anthropologist, in his exhaustive study of the origins of religious customs, mentions gods of rebirth. Adonis, the lover of Aphrodite, mysteriously appears in the world and then perishes in his youth. His blood has the magickal power of regeneration as the Fisher King. Tammuz, a Semitic deity, has much in common with Adonis. An etymological link, in that *Adonai* is the Hebrew word for "Lord," seems relevant here.

As already mentioned, the prime candidate for the origin of the figure of Jesus is the Roman god Mithras who, in turn, derives from the Persian *Mithra*. The significant commonality of the legends is demonstrated in the theme of a "virgin birth" and "divine light." This personification—of the god as a "giver of light," spiritual and fertile—is pertinent. Mithras is always depicted as being on high mountains or among the constellations. His symbol is a lion's head surrounded by the rays of the Sun—he returns with the dawn and brings light to the world.

The Mithras/Dionysius cult is particularly associated with the winter solstice, that point in the year when the Sun returns and vanquishes the powers of darkness. The death of Adonis/Arthur is a sacrifice to Aphrodite, incarnated in her dark persona as Morgan le Fay.

Dragon Queen

The dragon is a powerful symbol, with evocative descriptions of these wondrous creatures occurring in all cultures. The root of the word *dracon* is "to see clearly." It may be suggested that dragons are serpents with wings. Given that the serpent is accorded wisdom, its ability to fly gives it—like the eagle—the power of great sight or "insight." Uther Pendragon—the name means "Chief of Warriors"—was the father of Arthur.

The earliest devotees to dragon lore were the "Eleven Lords and Ladies of the Forest," a secret society. The Dragon Queen and the Grail King were part of this lore, their relationship having a similarity to the High Priestess and Priest. A later organization of the fifteenth century was the *Societas Draconis,* which included the kings of Poland and Aragon among its members. The Merovingian Kings of Gaul were also part of this arcane organization and there is a strong connection with the Cathars, as we shall discover.

Christianity presents the Archangel Michael as the symbol of light. He is the trusted servant of God, fulfilling his will. Churches built on mounds—such as that once perched upon Glastonbury Tor—are dedicated to him. In the esoteric, Michael is assigned to the element of Fire and the direction of the South. He wears a breast plate depicting the Sun at noon—the hour at its most powerful. Although Michael is depicted as slaying the serpent (or dragon), this is an exclusively Christian interpretation of the creature. It has become the Devil or a symbol of evil. A more positive interpretation is that Michael gains wisdom from the dragon in their encounter.

Kings are also associated with high places where they stand in order to survey their domain. Arthur as king/deity loves the earth, his very own clay, and he wishes to cherish and protect his inheritance. Several prominent landmarks in Britain, such as Arthur's Seat in Edinburgh, are associated both with the king and with dragon energy.

Among others, the dragon is given the quality of guarding treasure. It is said that the red light in the dragon's eyes reflects the wealth that it guards. Dragon's blood has the property of healing, and this may have correspondence with the blood of Christ, also having such a miraculous power. The two headed dragon, that extraordinary creature found in heraldic devices, represents a struggle between the conscious and the unconscious. The element of Fire, when manifest in the dragon, is the will when combined with courage and nobility. In myth, the dragon rules the skies and has the ability to swallow the Sun and the Moon, causing an eclipse.

On the subject of myth, we can do no better than reflect upon the insights of Joseph Campbell.

"Mythology has been interpreted…as a primitive, fumbling effort to explain the world of nature (Frazer); as a…poetical fantasy from prehistoric times…(Muller); as a repository of allegorical instruction, to shape the individual to his group (Durkheim); as a group dream, symptomatic of archetypal urges within the depths of the human psyche (Jung); as the…vehicle of…metaphysical insights (Comaraswamy); and as God's revelation to His children (the Church). Mythology is all of these…when scrutinized in terms not of what it is but of how it functions, of how it has served mankind in the past, of how it may serve today, mythology shows itself to be as amenable as life itself…"[20]

IV. THE QUEST

"WHAT IS THE GRAIL?
"FROM THE STANDPOINT OF THE WAY OF DUTY,
ANYONE IN EXILE FROM THE COMMUNITY IS A
NOTHING. FROM THE OTHER POINT OF VIEW,
HOWEVER, THIS EXILE IS THE FIRST STEP OF THE
QUEST."

— JOSEPH CAMPBELL

Why must the Grail be sought and then returned to the Grail Keeper? It is to restore the kingdom which has been devastated and become the Waste Land. What was once fertile and full of abundance has become sterile and devoid of life. This place of emptiness represents limbo, where faith has been abandoned and all seems purposeless. T.S. Eliot published his greatest work *The Waste Land* in 1922, a time when events in the world reflected a sense of hopelessness and many felt abandoned to an uncertain future.

"What are the roots that clutch, what branches grow
Out of this stony rubbish? Son of man,
You cannot say, or guess, for you know only
A heap of broken images..."[21]

Once the Grail Maidens tended the sacred cup and ensured that the waters of life continued to flow, nurturing all. The destruction of the kingdom and its fall is the result of the rapacity of man. King Amangon and his followers not only ravished the innocent Grail Maidens but stole their cup. The punishment for this crime was the refusal of the Goddess to nurture the land. Chosen as a symbolic victim, the impotent Fisher King waits in melancholy silence for deliverance to come.

The Grail Maidens, once in thrall of the Moon, know they cannot call upon her to bring the renewal that the Waste Land seeks. The power that is needed to redress the natural balance is not a passive lunar vibration, but another—one active and full of determination. The nature of the knight, resolute and resourceful, reflects the qualities essential to the Quest. The unrelenting search for the Grail and the joy met with at its discovery are the fundamental elements of the Quest. The restoring of the cup to its rightful place is the culmination of the noble task. Who better to gain this prize than the Company of the Round Table at King Arthur's court?

The Round Table

Conveniently, the company of knights arrived at Camelot at the same time as the Round Table. Earlier, Merlin had suggested to Leodegrance, the father of Guinevere, that this table should be the bride's dowry. He agreed and thus the Round Table became the nucleus of King Arthur's court. The circular design ensured that none sitting around it, apart from the king, would have precedence over another. Considering the belligerent temperament of fighting men, this was wise.

The association of Guinevere with the Round Table indicates the earthly, feminine nature it represents. Two examples of "sacred" tables precede it. One was the table around which Christ and the disciples gathered at the Last Supper. The other was a circular table on which the Grail was to be displayed, the heavenly behest given to Joseph of Arimathea. The Round Table also echoes the shape of a stone circle, and it is said that kings would be chosen from a select company gathered at these megalithic monuments. Stone circles at megalithic sites reflect the shape of the world, some even the stars and planets. Our ancestors intended these patterns of stones to be a reflection of the cosmos.

The Round Table appears to be the source of supernatural happenings that the Company who gather about it experiences. These events always involve some trial for the knights. Merlin is thus instrumental in setting up the Quest, the ultimate trial for any knight. When Merlin departs from the Arthurian tales, the Quest is over.

There are thirteen places at the Round Table. It is said that this number represents Christ and the Twelve Apostles. The thirteenth seat is referred to as the *Siege Perilous* and remains empty. Merlin has informed the Company that only a knight who has the right to secure the Grail may sit in the seat with impunity. If an unworthy candidate were to disobey this stricture, he would immediately incur the wrath of heaven and lose his life.

Two knights claim the honour of being the eventual keeper of the Grail—Sir Perceval and Sir Galahad. Sir Bors is also included in the company of those who set out to secure the Grail. Of the two candidates, Sir Perceval unknowingly occupies the "Perilous Seat" and is unharmed. Galahad also occupies the same seat, but, on this occasion, what occurs is markedly more dramatic. Arthur questions the knight to find out who he is and what has brought him to Camelot. Arthur is astonished when he discovers that Galahad's mother is Elaine, the daughter of King Pelles, the Fisher King. When Lancelot acknowledges that he is the youth's father, Arthur is yet even more astounded. According to Malory, Galahad took the seat exactly four hundred and fifty-four years after the death of Christ upon the Cross. Arthur immediately takes this as a sign that the Quest must begin.

The classic description of the Grail being revealed to the Company while seated at the Round Table demonstrates the exquisiteness of the event. Words are almost not enough to convey the glory of the scene.

"When they were all seated and the noise was hushed, there came a clap of thunder so loud and terrible they thought the palace must fall. Suddenly the hall was lit by a sunbeam which shed a radiance through the palace seven times brighter than had been before... They had sat a long while thus, unable to speak and gazing at one another like dumb animals. The Holy Grail appeared, covered with a cloth of white samite; and yet no mortal hand was seen to bear it. It entered through the great door, and at once the palace was filled with fragrance as though all the spices of the earth had been spilled abroad."[22]

A state of religious ecstasy is not exclusive to any one faith and there is no reason why a similar state cannot be also experienced in the secular world. Such a transcendental condition is the ultimate in being involved in the moment. There is no awareness of anything other than what is venerated. Motionless and unable to communicate with others, the subject experiences an otherworldly state which may be either very brief or prolonged for some time.

The Buddha's state of ecstasy reportedly continued for two weeks. The Western Magickal Tradition does not specifically cater to this kind of exercise, but for the initiate, the door to the Inner Planes has already been opened. The Eastern tradition regards the state of ecstasy as the goal of all religious practice. Though bound by the Grail ethic, the knights upon the Quest are also deliberately searching for the same experience.

Chivalry

In medieval times, a knight wielded enormous power. On the battlefield, he was a dealer of death to the foot soldiers of the enemy who eddied about in the wake of his armored steed. In a later period, the Code of Chivalry (*chevalier*—horse man) modified and directly influenced the mores of the knight. The chivalric tradition originates in the East among the Bedouins and then migrated to medieval Spain—a country referred to as "the cradle of chivalry." The qualities the Arab knight was expected to own were loyalty, courtesy, and munificence. The Spanish tradition added piety, courtesy, eloquence, and mastering the art of poetry.

Chivalry came to be understood as a moral and social code of conduct. It was an idealized version of the life of a knight who was expected to adhere to the virtues of courage, honour, and service. Chivalry is also associated with a state of mind, one that is heroic yet conversant with aesthetic values and the purity of the intellect. Such a model of conduct later gave rise to the rank of gentleman or courtier. The subject has a high standard of etiquette and his conduct adheres to the strictest principles.

Given this fixed code of living, any quandary for the noble knight would have revolved about the purpose of his life—one almost existential. It would have been a traumatic experience for any knight to suddenly doubt the very basis of his calling. To be faced with the realization that existence might be ultimately meaningless is the greatest trauma for any one of us. Such a moment may be utterly and totally devastating and, in an Arthurian context, could even result in the death of the knight.

In Cervantes' *Don Quixote*, we encounter that extraordinary Spanish gentleman who, obsessed by his reading about chivalry, sets out to be a noble knight. The tale introduces all manner of strange escapades and convoluted emotions. Surprisingly perhaps, given its reputation as a comic piece, it does reveal certain insights into the nature of the Grail Quest.

Don Quixote's behaviour is reckless and often ill-conceived, yet he cannot view the world in any way but his own. The tragedy in the tale is that of a man of independent thought being forced to surrender his idiosyncratic vision. After his escapades, when Don Quixote eventually returns to civilization, there is no alternative for him but to adopt the mantle of sanity—the dull conformity insisted upon by society. His conscious view during his quest has been of the glory of chivalry, leavened by the knowledge that it is an unreal pursuit. He is a believer who does not believe, and in perceiving this, he has great knowledge, though he is regarded as a simpleton and a fool.

In contrast, the Arthurian knights, volubly dedicated to their cause, often display what might be regarded as psychotic or manic tendencies. Their behaviour is often a reaction to overwhelming emotions, their lives being lived for the most part "on the edge." Is this a reflection of the medieval zeitgeist? We see this as a chaotic panorama—violent death, extreme piety, great doubt, and hardship. Is the search for the Grail made even more fervent because it promises sublime tranquility? Will it be a rest from strife—one that the life of the man of the Middle Ages lacked?

Galahad and Gawain

For the knights, the Quest is no sinecure. Only one of the Company is successful in finding the Grail, and who that is—whether Perceval or Galahad—depends upon which version of the tale is read. Perceval features in the versions of the Grail legends told by Chrétien de Troyes, Wolfram von Eschenbach, and Robert de Boron. These authors provide the bulk of the Arthurian canon. Sir Gawain features prominently in another work, *Diou Crone,* and Galahad appears in the *Vulgate Cycle.* These two works are helpful in providing additional insights into the Arthuriad.

It is instructive to contrast these three knights—Galahad, Perceval, and Gawain. What is it that makes this triumvirate memorable over the rather flat characters that comprise the rest of the Company? Sir Perceval, either the cousin of Sir Lancelot or his loyal companion, is the naïve youth who is permitted to enter Carbonek, the Grail Castle. He is then too overawed by the sight of the Grail to ask the Grail Question— "Whom does the Grail serve?"

Galahad is said to have such a purity of heart that his only passion in life is to discover the Grail. His sense of being "the chosen one" never leaves him for a moment and spurs him on during the Quest. He is an enigmatic and unworldly figure, one almost impossible to believe exists. It is also difficult not to regard the *parfait knight* without some air of suspicion or even resentment. Why does Galahad have a monopoly on owning the holy vessel? Surely the Grail is within all of us.

Sir Gawain can be seen as essentially a Pagan character transformed into a Christian knight. The tale "Sir Gawain and the Green Knight" is another Medieval morality tale. It revolves around Gawain's rebuttal of the advances made upon him by the beautiful wife of Bertilak de Hautdesert, who is revealed as the "Green Knight" of the title. Gawain is lodging in the latter's castle and while his host is away, the lady enters the young knight's bedchamber. Sir Gawain's refusal to be tempted by her charms is seen as proof of his loyalty to the vows of chastity essential to his knightly calling.

Lancelot

Sir Lancelot was raised by the Lady of the Lake, hence his appellation *du Lac*. He is the father of Galahad and the lover of Arthur's queen. Steeped in mortal sin (according to the Grail ethos), he is not worthy to behold more than a fleeting glimpse of the Holy of Holies. While visiting Castle Carbonek, engaged in his Quest, another woman falls under his spell. She is Elaine, the daughter of Pelles and a Grail Bearer. She confesses her passion to another of the maidens, who then provide Elaine with the magickal means to gain Lancelot's attention. She is able to assume the appearance of Guinevere.

Unaware that the woman in his bedchamber is not his true love, Lancelot sleeps with her. The fruit of their union is a son, Galahad, the only knight who succeeds in possessing the Grail. But we may enquire, only the pure are permitted to possess the Grail, so how can this be? The rather convoluted answer is this: Although Galahad is illegitimate, Elaine was a virgin before she met Lancelot. Apparently, this is enough reason for letting her son claim the requisite purity. The medieval mind moves in mysterious ways its wonders to perform!

The bridge is a symbol of passing from one world to another. In the Norse tradition, *Bifrost*—the Rainbow Bridge—leads from *Midgard*, the world of mortals, to *Asgard*, the realm of the gods. Lancelot has to cross the *Bridge of Swords* in order to rescue Guinevere, and Perceval braves the *pont de voirre*—the Bridge of Crystal. In both instances, each is given a magickal ring. This bestows upon the wearer the strength of mind needed to combat the demons within and fend off the demons without.

In the Greek tradition, the river Styx marked the division between Earth and the Underworld. The Arthurian tales cite the river Brue, a waterway in Somerset that once marked the coast of the Isle of Avalon. Here is located Brides Mound, or Beckery (from the Irish *beag Eiru*—little Ireland), or perhaps *bheach haorai*, mound of the bees. It is in the chapel, built on this holy place, that the knights rest before the final stage of their pilgrimage. In the dawn, they cross the *Pons Perilis* before the journey that leads them to the Grail Castle, wherein lies the sacred prize.

Beholding the Invisible

Whether we desire it or not, from the moment we enter this world, we have embarked upon a Quest. Whether an individual comes to regard their life in this light is a matter for destiny to decide. However, reflecting upon the human condition and the "whither are we bound," has always been a preoccupation of man. From the time that he became *homo sapiens* and acquired the ability to conceptualize, he has wondered about the purpose of his existence. We ask ourselves how we should best employ the span of life allotted to each one of us. Or do we follow Shakespeare's rather melancholy assessment,

> *"Life's but a walking shadow, a poor player*
> *That struts and frets his hour upon the stage*
> *And then is heard no more. It is a tale*
> *Told buy an idiot, full of sound and fury,*
> *Signifying nothing."*

The "human" part of ourselves sends us on a mission to find the spiritual element within us. We are sent tasks in order to take us out of the darkness of ignorance and into the light of understanding. It is not merely "knowledge," an accumulation of facts, or even heaven that we seek, but the fullness of comprehension. We constantly observe "through a glass darkly," and it is this total reappraisal of how we perceive that is the purpose of the Quest.

The tradition of the individual following his own spiritual path originates with the Greeks—Jason or Heracles being the most celebrated examples. This classical approach was overthrown by the Judaic and later Christian promotion of the "corporate identity." By the time of the flowering of the Grail (1150-1250), this stance had changed once again and the communal approach no longer found favour. In Malory's Arthur will be found a telling passage:

> *"...each entered the forest at a point that he, himself, had chosen, where it was darkest and there was no path."*[23]

One might conclude from such a view that Parzival fails in his endeavours because he strictly adheres to the party line and does not follow his own intuition.

Whether their journey is undertaken with a companion or not, those upon it inevitably encounter doubt and loneliness on the way. Everything that was previously considered safe and secure is torn away and the realization that there is nothing to hold onto comes about. It is at that moment enlightenment begins. When we are shaken to the core, we discover exactly what lies within that core.

The Perslesvaus is supposedly a continuation by an unknown author of Chrétien de Troye's account of Perceval. In it, Arthur is the last member of the Round Table to see the Grail in the West. In a sequence of five visions, three are related to kingship and Christ, one is obscured, and the final image is of the chalice. It is then unclear from the texts whether Galahad conveys the Grail to Sarras. The reason for its departure, however, is made abundantly clear—man is not worthy of its keeping. Logres, the scared kingdom that played host to the Grail, has descended into chaos and anarchy.

Idyllic kingdoms like Atlantis or Lemuria only have a finite existence. Perhaps a more plausible case for a "lost continent," one even more ancient, was the "Land of Mu," supposedly twelve thousand years old. Some authorities maintain that the peoples of Egypt, Greece, and India originated from here. According to Augustus Le Plongeon, an English antiquarian and photographer of Mayan civilization, it was situated in the western part of the Atlantic Ocean.

V. ALTERED STATES

"TO FATHOM HELL OR SOAR ANGELIC
JUST TAKE A PINCH OF PSYCHEDELIC."

— HUMPHREY OSMOND

Everything that the senses perceive is a part of human consciousness. A heightened sensitivity is supposedly a result of being in the presence of the holy vessel. Is it possible, by altering our consciousness, to *induce* a sensitivity so finely tuned that it replicates the experience of the knights upon their Quest? What was most assuredly possible in the twentieth century and before were the means for an individual to undergo an altered state.

The capability within the human brain is truly extraordinary. A pinhead of DNA has the capacity to store the information contained in a pile of books five hundred times as tall as the distance from the Earth to the Moon. The brain is a billion times better equipped than the hard drive of any computer. In relaying information, the brain has the advantage over any electronic device because it possesses a more complex mode of operation. The brain has trillions of connections between its cells and is thus capable of performing countless operations simultaneously. The brain is an organ like any other in the body. The "mind" is a convenient way of describing the sensations that occur when the brain is in operation. A distinction lies between "consciousness" and "perception." The former applies to a state of experiencing existence, the latter to the mechanics of a particular phenomenon within that experience.

How do we "perceive" anything? Understanding the mechanics of perception has always been a problem for cognitive science. This area of the brain's activity is regarded by scientists as being almost akin to a jungle, one with almost unfathomable depths and no boundaries. How does the brain sort, codify, and draw meaning from the information it receives from the senses? Not only that, but perception also includes the ability to recognize, detect, and understand.

This "ability to understand" is crucial to engaging with the transcendental idea that the Grail so obviously is. To "know" through experiencing the holy vessel is not enough—we yearn to gain wisdom from it. This is the ambition of the true thinker. Thus, with our brains, we desire to completely comprehend an idea on every possible level and with every possible implication. We expect to be able to access concepts, assess a situation as a coherent whole, and grasp all the abstract relations within it. If we do not achieve these things, then we consider that the brain is functioning at a low level of perception.

Perception has the result of producing a mental representation. The process of forming these representations is complex and is the source of much debate among neuroscientists. If "representation" does not occur, then impressions that are received have no structure or organization—they are virtually useless. Unfiltered information cannot be used for any useful purpose; it simply remains random.

How does context affect our representations? In what way do we radically reassess a situation? What methods do we use in referring to previously assimilated concepts? And by far the most important question is: how does the quality that we refer to as "understanding" emerge from all this?

One possible solution to all of these questions is that we constantly create analogies. The act of constructing these "representations" may account for how we actually perceive things. Analogical thought may, however, occur at the same time as perception—thus, *ipso facto*, there is no difference between the two processes. Analogy cannot exist without perception and perception includes the function of analogy. It appears that one is a metaphor for the other.

Plato saw analogy as shared abstraction. Abstraction is an intrinsic part of perception, so we would expect that analogous objects would share certain qualities—ones that we were able to detect. These qualities include pattern, function, or attribute—all elements that facilitate our understanding. Plato also held the view that information was never lost; it was simply relocated, waiting patiently until it was later retrieved. We are able to employ some gobbet of information over and over again, then abandoning it each time after we have examined it.

It is also apparent that every atom in the universe contains information. We may conclude that objects require "instructions" to assemble themselves into recognizable forms. A table appears as it does because the atoms that fill this "table space" are working in cooperation to create the appearance of a table. They need not remain static; physics actually tells us that atoms are constantly in motion. They may also appear to change their identity, for instance, if the table suddenly collapses.

The Grail is composed of atoms like anything else, and as observers of the holy vessel, we are as well. We will have a conception of how it may appear. Eastern teachings promote a view that by attachment to fixed ideas that our senses have told us exist, we inhabit a world of illusion. Better to accept that all is in endless motion, a constant state of flux, and everything is in a dynamic relationship with everything else. Nothing can have an immutable essence because it is part of a cosmic emptiness. The void is the "space" in which we create objects because we desire them to be there. In Tibetan art, the visual analogy is that of the sky. The clouds only exist so that we may have something to hang onto in all this eternity.

Transference of information from one synapse to another—
the verbal or visual relaying of ideas—relies upon the action of
atoms. Our means of communication, from the most advanced
technological hardware to a simple conversation, still rely on an
interchange of energy. As individual human beings, we use different
concepts of language to express the same idea. The two extreme
modes of understanding are relativism and solipsism. Relativism
denotes that the truth is decided by a single observation, the
solipsistic approach involves the individual being the sole legislator
of all reality. The drawback of both approaches is easily perceived.

Although we all sense things differently, we often behave as if we
share a common perception. Such is the value of discussion and the
sharing of ideas. If we do not do this, our thinking becomes rigid;
metaphorically, our synapses atrophy. We rely on the imagination to
create perceptions, giving meaning to experience and understanding
from knowledge. One way in which we make sense of all this is to
permit alteration and correction of our concepts.

The Grail, because it is beyond the material—in a sphere that
is divorced from merely *ideas of the spiritual*—is limitless in its
application. It contains all ideas, all wisdom, and every possible
manner of perception.

By discovering the Grail within ourselves—our true selves—we
also discover our true perceptions.

Dreams

On February 9th 1856, Lewis Carroll wrote in his diary:

> *"...when we are dreaming and, as often happens, have a dim
> consciousness of the fact and try to wake, do we not say and do things
> which in waking life would be insane? May we not then sometimes
> define insanity as an inability to distinguish which is the waking
> and which is the sleeping life?"*[24]

On their journey, the knights see visions of the Grail in their
dreams. Sometimes these are revelations of a particular direction,
spiritual or actual, that they must take upon the way—the more

vivid the vision, the more overwhelming the experience for the dreamer. The image of the holy vessel becomes more powerful the more intensely it is being sought after. The power of dreams is that they create a gateway between two worlds, the outer and the inner.

This is the "luminous mind," referred to by the writers in the East. The same phenomenon in psychology is referred to as *psi.* The term denotes the "processing of information," an activity dear to Americans. Defining what is known as an "altered state" often relies upon the concept of psi. Data stored in the brain, information that is either ignored or hidden deep in the unconscious, may be suddenly and dramatically released. On another level, it is an actual transfer of energy, linked with phenomena such as telepathy and the paranormal.

Freud suggests that in the dream state, we embrace "primary process" thoughts and seek to manifest what resides in the psyche. What he termed "secondary process" thoughts seek to inhibit the flow of psychic energy and return it to a state of reason. A more modern view suggests that, during sleep, the pineal gland releases chemicals which create for us a hallucinogenic state of mind. This would explain why our dreams own a different "reality."

The actual substance cited is dimethyltryptamine (DMT). Though it may be synthesized in the laboratory, it occurs in a natural state in many plants. DMT is a potent psychedelic drug and brings about hallucinogenic experiences. The same drug is produced in small amounts by the body during its normal metabolism. Our "everyday reality" may actually be dictated by the continual action of this process. Is our conscious world nothing more than a controlled psychedelic trip?

If the "control mechanisms" in the brain do not operate correctly, a truly "altered state" arises, one that is divorced from "familiar" reality. This certainly strengthens the view, one held by mystics for centuries, that consciousness exists outside of the body and is totally independent of it. This implies that man has no control over his perceptions and cannot create a reality that suits him. If he does convince himself that he has created a reality solely his own, society regards him as either a magician or a madman!

What is known as "lucid dreaming" may be regarded as a halfway house between dream reality and ordinary reality. Here, the dreamer actively directs what happens in his dream. It was said that in ancient times, man was once capable—by the means of using his "third eye,"—to enter the otherworld whenever he so wished. Some believe this facility will soon become part of our common consciousness once more. When this occurs, man will be in a position to interact with his fellow beings on more than one level. He will even have the power of communicating with extra-terrestrial beings with the greatest of ease.

Of predictions concerning how man will utilize his brain in the future, physicist Freeman Dyson proposes that:

> *"Although the physical time necessary to think and process information may be spread out over billions of years, the 'subjective time,' as seen by the intelligent creatures themselves, will remain the same. They will never notice the difference. They will still be able to think deep thoughts but only on a much, much slower time scale...Processing a single thought may take trillions of years, but with respect to 'subjective time,' thinking will proceed normally."[25]*

Such a view is very akin to the belief that the year 2012 would have brought a great "shift" of consciousness to the planet. It was a view shared by many who cite the "Mayan prophecies," the Book of Revelation, and phenomena such as crop circles as incontrovertible proof.

It is the vexed question of the validity of our perceptions that is at stake, and we must examine how the brain operates. It has the ability to store an incredible number of memories in a small space, so does it operate holographically? The ability to retrieve information so quickly indicates a cross-correlated system. Does this explain how the brain converts external stimuli into perceptual responses? Karl H. Pribram's thesis is that a "hard" reality is constructed and various frequencies or types of sensory input are sorted into conventions of understanding. The key word here is "conventions." How do our conceptions of time and space relate to what really "exists"?

Much that we accept as "reality" is merely habit. Our understanding is limited, our view subjective. Is it all merely *Maya*—illusion—as Eastern philosophy has always maintained?

If consciousness is regarded as a continuum, it is then connected to every other consciousness that exists or has ever existed. An eternal, infinite, and ultimately sympathetic world has at its heart the Grail—embracing all that has been or ever will be. Yet we might speculate that the Grail exists only in an eternal present.

"Reality" is more often than not a consensus of what is happening, one formulated by ourselves and others. Castaneda's *Don Juan* speaks of this:

> "Let's say that when every one of us is born we bring with us a little ring of power. That little ring is almost immediately put to use. So every one of us is already hooked from birth and our rings of power are joined to everyone else's. In other words, our rings of power are hooked to the doing of the world in order to make the world."[26]

It may be that our well-being, both physical and spiritual, is dependent upon how we imagine ourselves to be at any given time. To manifest a positive state of mind, we must be constantly aware of our personal power. Magick is not something that only certain individuals are capable of performing; it is all around us and within us, for everything is a metaphor of experience.

When we dream or meditate, we are in accord with the belief of the Ancient Egyptians that we live simultaneously on no fewer than nine dimensions. Many of these are non-physical and can only be attained through dreaming, but even that state has a degree of reality as relevant as the one we experience upon waking. This is the "gap between worlds" where magick exists, the space in which the shaman operates.

Opening the Doors

From 1940 onward, much research was carried out into the effects of a variety of hallucinogenic substances. The first drug to be seriously examined was mescaline. Its effect of inducing a state similar to schizophrenia encouraged psychologists to continue with investigations into its properties. Since the beginning of the twentieth century, Freud had maintained that taking hallucinogenic drugs was a method of opening up the unconscious.

At the same time various theories were proposed, including Freud's, as to the nature of that unconscious. It was suggested that the unconscious had four parts: the unconscious memory, the repressive memory, the creative urge, and the mythopoetic—the realm of archetypes. It was this last area that fascinated Jung and gave rise to his idea of the collective unconscious. This is the abode of the archetypes, the Arthurian figures being some of the most impressive.

At the same time, psychologists were particularly interested in what "reality" was. Would the experiences that occurred after taking mescaline or peyote throw light on our understanding of what "the real" is? The more enlightened researchers realised how akin this seeking after "truth" was to the practice, always prevalent in the East, of seeking "cosmic" consciousness. At the beginning of the 1960s, religious dogma was not popular, but the pursuit of spirituality and ways of suggesting a means for spiritual evolution were welcomed.

Even prior to this period, thinkers in the West had realised that "mystical experience" was an impressive phenomenon, one not to be lightly dismissed. Some even proposed that a new system of education could be introduced, one that considered spiritual awareness as a realistic goal for students. One of the problems encountered, however, was that Western forms were often highly unsuited as a medium for instruction in spiritual matters. The language of the East appeared to be far more suited for such a purpose. Sanskrit, for instance, had forty different words for a change in consciousness.

A New Trip

In the 1950s, investigations of mind-altering substances were confined to the properties of psychotropic mushrooms found in Mexico. In 1938, however, Albert Hoffman had successfully synthesized a hallucinogenic substance. This was lysergic acid diethylamide (LSD), a compound known as LSD 25. By 1947, this had been successfully synthesized in appreciable quantities by the Sandoz laboratories in Switzerland. LSD was then available for use by researchers in psychology departments in several universities in America. What was interesting was that many of the resultant records of these investigations were couched in spiritual terms. In these reports, words like "eternal" and "infinity" were quite common.

What is the "psychedelic" experience? It has been described countless times and often at great length. The "endless trip" is itself an accurate description of some of the extraordinarily detailed accounts of this state. It is a truism that words are inadequate to describe what occurs, but for our purposes, *"the experiencing of states of awareness or consciousness profoundly different from the usual waking consciousness"* will suffice.[27]

Research into psychedelics, coming as it did at the same time as the development of computers and artificial intelligence, seemed to indicate that the human brain was far in advance of any mechanism that technology could produce. What is also evident from contemporary texts is the extremely responsible attitude of those of those who were involved in research into psychedelics. Many highly respected members of the scientific establishment believed LSD would be of major benefit to mankind.

In the 1960s, Dr. Robert Masters inaugurated "The Foundation for Mind Research" in New York. His work was highly respected by therapists and academics, among them Stanislav Grof and Joseph Campbell. Masters was a pioneer of methods that he believed would break down boundaries between areas of consciousness. He was convinced that to bring about a real understanding of the way we see things, new ways of perception were desperately needed. He believed that old and outmoded patterns of thought held us back. Masters believed that if this radical change could occur, we would experience:

> *"...a world that has slipped the chains of normal categorical ordering. A vast range of phenomena normally excluded enter in the extended consciousness. The mind no longer is subject to the highly selective censorship or screening usually imposed upon it by the ordinarily dominant mechanisms of the newest (cortical) areas of the brain. Mechanisms much older in evolutionary terms become dominant. Novel experiences and a wealth of other experiences then become possible."*[28]

Masters was convinced that with the advancement of scientific thinking, mankind needed a brain that would operate on new levels. Combined with this was his individual vision for a more cogent and sympathetic system of psychotherapy. To him, the two worlds were not exclusive. The following statement was written by him in 1967.

It is a sober and sane plea, one in direct contrast to the subsequent media hysteria that would erupt around "psychedelic drugs."

> *"On the basis of our experience—a combined fifteen years of research with LSD, peyote, and other psychedelics—we believe that LSD-type chemicals provide the best access yet to the contents and processes of the human mind. They have value in psychotherapy, but also for research in many areas outside medicine and therapy—for example, philosophy, psychology, anthropology, religion, scientific problem solving, and the arts—and research with normal persons probably will yield results of ultimately greater value than the therapeutic uses. We favor greatly expanded research programs unburdened by excessive bureaucratic interference but subject to periodic evaluations to determine that the work is responsible and that risks have been minimized."[29]*

At the same time that Masters was conducting his investigations, a certain Harvard professor was causing some disquiet among his colleagues for his unconventional approach to psychological research.

Turning On

Until he was fired in 1963, Timothy Leary was a university professor with a sparkling career in front of him. A few years later, he was to voluntarily become the acid guru of the counterculture. He will be forever associated with the 60s mantra— "Turn on, tune in, drop out." If we remove these sentiments from the context of flower-power rhetoric, a different interpretation emerges. Leary maintained that he spoke of another, far older, tradition.

> *"Turn on means to go beyond your secular tribal mind to contact the many levels of divine energy which lie within your consciousness; tune in means to express and to communicate your new revelations in visible acts of glorification, gratitude and beauty; drop out means to detach yourself harmoniously, tenderly and gracefully from worldly commitments until your entire life is dedicated to worship and search."[30]*

Together, Leary and Richard Alpert, another Harvard professor, founded a community they named Millbrook. They continued with their experimentation and Leary quickly became a high-profile exponent of the "psychedelic lifestyle." Alpert, meanwhile, went to India and embraced a more conventional spiritual path. Leary subsequently fell afoul of American law-enforcement agencies and was arrested for drug possession. He was seen by the moral majority in America as a dangerous influence on youth.

It cannot be denied that a great quantity of LSD has been imbibed since the 1960s, not for reasons of high-minded research, but for recreational purposes. Although "acid" was made illegal both in the UK and USA in 1966, the following year will always be known as "The Summer of Love." Apart from the obvious sexual connotations, 1967 has always been associated, for a great many people—many famous—with taking their first "trip."[31]

A definite lifestyle developed around the "acid" experience. Posters, music, magazines, and "underground" clubs outwardly reflected the trend. Colourful clothes and long hair were the badge of identity for those who had embraced the psychedelic culture. Most of the older generation were merely bemused by the moustaches, long hair, kaftans, and beads. However, many artists and intellectuals added their own contribution to a growing change in consciousness. It was one that they applauded, or at least felt they could not ignore.

Whether the "drug culture" or some other catalyst was responsible for real social change is a matter for the sociologist and cultural historian. It is easy to be content with a stereotyped view of the Sixties, which is to misunderstand much. A great deal has been written about the decade, very little of it providing any answers as to how, or indeed why, things happened as they did. The adage that "you had to be there" is undeniably relevant.

Is the drug experience, or more specifically, imbibing LSD, in any way akin to the Quest? The question might seem heretical to the Arthurian scholar, but having a greater remit in our study, we may wish to examine its relevance. When discussing the effects of LSD, Dr. Masters remarked that, *"A result can be the breaching of the walls that ordinarily separate conscious and unconscious minds."*[32] That sentiment is perfectly in accord with the enlightenment promised by the Grail.

Let us, with a cool eye, first examine the nature of drugs. In the West, we accept certain substance such as caffeine and alcohol, although they are potent stimulants, as being socially acceptable. Other cultures do not do so—the Muslim religion forbids the consumption of alcohol.

In ancient times, many societies embraced the hallucinogenic drug experience as part of a generic culture of enlightenment. The West has always been more prone to regarding certain drugs, but not others, as dangerous and harmful. Even in British folk culture, henbane and *amanita muscaria* were regarded as only fit for the witches' cauldron, never part of any formalized, social ritual.

Highs and Lows

We refer once more to Lewis Carroll in attempting to discover the reasons for man's continuing fascination with the fabric of reality and how it may be altered. Martin Gardner questions the way Carroll's psyche was evoked in his works.

> *"...whether there were unconscious compulsions that made it necessary for him to be forever warping and stretching, compressing and inverting, reversing and distorting the familiar world."*[33]

A quixotic stance in the twenty-first century simultaneously condemns and accepts widespread drug use and abuse in our culture. There are more than a quarter of a million heroin addicts in the UK and nearly a million in the USA—this is not a comforting statistic.

The greatest danger of regarding drugs as the *only* gateway to enlightenment is that they are so obviously a diversion—a "red herring" as we might say. The more time that elapses when one is diverted from the path, the greater the chance of error. The warning of Sri Krishna Prem, an Englishman living the spiritual life in India, is apposite.

> *"Drugs are the most influential and dangerous powers available to humans. They open up glorious and pleasurable chambers in the mind. They give great power. Thus they can seduce the searcher away from the Path."*[34]

Meditation, study, and ritual are the pathways to enlightenment. There is no shortcut to this end. The only other parallel between drugs and the Grail is that of completely losing the "self." The concept of the *ego* has only existed since it was postulated by Freud, and one wonders if it is a case of *cogito ergo sum*. The reference to "I" that we constantly make is a misnomer, and if we constantly reinforce this notion of "our self," we are led into grave errors of perception. We are what we think we are, but we need not be deluded by the assumption that we have to play a part, as an actor does. The mistake is to assume that the *persona* is the same as the personality. There is no "I."

According to quantum physics, the observer has a significant affect upon what is observed. We may suggest that this is an inevitable result of various elements being in the same location in time and space. Atoms have combined and interact. We begin to enter the world beyond the visible—that limitless existence not consciously perceived. Perhaps the current preoccupation with the Grail suggests that there is a growing awareness of this "otherworld." The use of drugs as a means of "mind expansion" in the 1960s was an indication that a change of consciousness was dawning, but it was a false dawn.

Our dreams, using a vocabulary and language of their own, are a way we have to communicate with our own inner selves. In dreams, shifts in reality seem perfectly plausible. Wittgenstein insisted that the limits of our discourse were maintained by the limits of language. We could postulate that the limits of our perception are equally restricted by the boundaries of our imagination. We must learn, as Keats suggests, to *ever let the fancy roam.*

VI. COSMIC TIME

"IT WAS FOUR IN THE AFTERNOON,
ALTHOUGH TO TELL THE TRUTH, A WATCH IS
UNCONCERNED, IT GOES FROM ONE TO TWELVE,
THE REST ARE IDEAS IN THE MIND."

— JOSE SARAMAGO

Time flows, space contains. These are workable definitions, but we conclude that they are merely constructs and have no real meaning. Thinking that "time" bonds us to the material world may make us feel more secure in our environment, but any such belief is illusory. If we wish to remove such constraints to our understanding, we had best deny the existence of time as an entity. Lewis Carroll, apart from entertaining us, raises some interesting issues in *Alice in Wonderland*.

> *'Alice sighed wearily. 'I think you might do something better with time,' she said, 'than wasting it in asking riddles that have no answers.'*
>
> *'If you knew Time as well as I do,' said the Hatter, 'you wouldn't talk about wasting it. It's him.'*

'I don't know what you mean,' said Alice.

'Of course you don't!' the Hatter said, tossing his head contemptuously. 'I dare say you have never even spoken to Time!'

'Perhaps not,' Alice cautiously replied; 'but I know I beat time when I learn music.'

'Ah! That accounts for it,' said the Hatter. 'He won't stand beating. Now, if you only kept on good terms with him, he'd do almost anything you liked with the clock. For instance, suppose it were nine o'clock in the morning, just time to begin lessons; you'd only have to whisper a hint to Time, and round goes the clock in a twinkling! Half-past one, time for dinner!'

Determinism, a view held for thousands of years, propounded that what occurs in the universe is no more than a chain of events, one following the other in an endless succession of cause and effect. By the beginning of the eighteenth century, this view was being questioned. David Hume dismissed determinism as, *"the spurious offspring of the imagination, impregnated by custom."* He also went on to say that:

"The supposition that the future resembles the past is not founded on arguments of any kind but is derived entirely from habit."[35]

Past, Present, and Future

We shall hear much of Einstein in our later discussion of "space-time." At present, we will be content with accepting his maintaining that time was a psychological construct. The brain was aware of a series of concurrent moments and regarded that experience as "time." David Deutsch considered different times to be different universes. *"The universes we can affect we call the future. Those that can affect us we call the past."*[36]

We have already heard something of altered states of consciousness. These are often characterized by a completely different estimation of how we "normally" regard time. To those experiencing such a state, the most accurate chronometer may appear to be a useless tool. The "passage of time" is meaningless because they are not experiencing it. Time may appear to slow down, speed up, or even travel backwards. Events may not conform to any idea of a linear sequence. The concept of a particular point in time, midnight or 7:00 a.m., has no relevance. Thus, we learn that time is best regarded as an abstraction, not something that directly affects us.

What other experiences do we encounter that may make us doubt whether "time" exists? When we experience a state of intense emotion is one such occasion. It may be that immense joy when lovers are entirely absorbed in each other, seeing only the brilliance in each other's eyes. When this occurs, the rest of the world appears to fade away. Such intensity creates the total experience of "the moment." It is a feeling that nothing else matters, and for lovers, ultimately, it does not. They are living in an eternal "now," a state that has no beginning and no end.

The negative aspect of experiencing "time" is as a weight about us—one that moves interminably slowly. The minutes and hours appear to drag relentlessly on, and we lose hope of achieving the goals we desperately wish for.

The "present" may be thought of a state where recollection and speculation do not exist. The idea of an "eternal present" is very ancient and was remarked upon by the first scholars. The indigenous population of Australia regards "time" as being a space in which one may move in any direction. If time is infinite and eternal, everything has already happened, and what is happening now will at some point recur.

The "past" only exists as an idea in the mind; it is impossible for us to experience the past in the present. To "relive" a previous event requires the action of the brain; only neuro-electrical impulses can create the past. Even the notion of "time-travel" has within it certain concepts that govern what is possible. The subject is too extensive to be dealt with here, but we may mention certain principles that are implicit within it.

How far one may travel into the past is determined by the moment when the time machine is created. The device itself moves through time, rather than the technology that created it being transported to a previous point. Travelling into the future is determined by "subjective" time. The length of time taken by the individual's journey will be in a different frame of reference to the place he visits. His journey may have taken a year, while the amount of time that has passed on Earth may be a hundred years. In this way, he is, in theory, able to travel into the future.

The only problem in the above scenario is that of attempting to predict the time reference. There is no objective answer to this, and it can only be added to the various unknowns around "time." Travelling through "wormholes" in the fabric of the universe may eliminate the paradoxes of time travel—such as meeting one's grandfather and other oft-quoted examples.

Strange Times

The onset of creation, the impelling of all action, is told as fable in all religious traditions. The opening words of the Bible are, *"In the beginning was the Word."* The same sentiment is embodied in the *Vach* of the Hindus, the *Beth-Kol* of Judaism, and the *Bhagavad-Gita* of the Hindus. The ancients referred to that moment as the "Soundless Sound"—the divine source from which all emerges.

It seems that there would have been "a time before time existed," estimated as being 13.7 billion years ago, before the "Big Bang." Our conceptions of time have been honed by society since then. We are subject to "local time," calculations are made in "sidereal time," and the world constantly refers to "Greenwich Mean Time."

We describe time in terms that give it a reality, even a life. We speak of the "time being right," "time being against us," and insist that "time flies." We have a myriad of expressions that refer to a phenomenon that we never completely understand, or perhaps even consider. By observing the physical changes that occur around us, we assume there is a "passing of time."

We seek to be, if not the masters of the universe, at least masters of time, wishing to preserve experiences that give us pleasure and fulfillment, for instance. How we spend our time is our own decision, yet the way in which we actually experience a moment, or an hour, is dependent upon something else—our interpretation and our mood.

An impassioned passage in the writings of Heidegger describes time as "vacillating," "paralyzing," and "torturing." Certainly, the idea of time dragging itself along almost like a wounded animal, holding us in a tedious limbo, is a powerful image. We cannot deal with time when it appears to stretch into a single state of "nowness," not flowing, but remaining always frozen and immobile.

Can we make time disappear? If we have decided that neither time nor space exists, we are moving into the realm of metaphysics. The philosopher moves into areas of speculation that do not solely rely upon observation; therefore, he works in a different realm than the scientist.

Isaac Newton proposed that "true time" was not affected by external influences. Woody Allen joked that "Time is nature's way of keeping everything from happening at once." Deciding that hours, days, and years are separate units does not help us to understand time. It is possible with the aid of atomic clocks to measure time so accurately that only an error of one second occurs in several million years. But a clock in deep space runs slower than any chronometer does on Earth...

The ultimate concern for most of us is in knowing when the sands of time will run out. Will we have "enough time" to complete what we set out to do? If we fear death, it is because we fear change. When we cease to fear death, we are able to see that all the changes in our lives are part of a constantly changing cycle. As something within us dies, something else is reborn. Death is not an end; it is a beginning. The Tarot card entitled *Death* depicts a Sun on the horizon. Whether it is rising or setting we cannot tell—neither state means more than the other.

We should attempt to understand Einstein's theory that space and duration are the same. "Light years" is a device developed to measure the vast distances that are impossible to calculate on a linear basis. The light from the Sun takes eight minutes to reach us on Earth. If our forefathers had been informed of this fact, they would have been at loss to see its relevance to their lives. They would have observed the passage of the Sun and the Moon across the sky but would not have considered the space between either of these bodies and the Earth as anything particularly significant. Their lives were ordered by the seasons, and thus they saw themselves as existing as part of a cycle that continued to occur, irrespective of any arbitrary notion of time.

To the universe, the notion of time is ridiculous! How could it be otherwise? From the vast storehouse of ideas that makes up ancient culture originates the Grail. The ancients would not have recognised any division between the mythical and the literal, their concepts of mathematics or medicine being as much aligned to the supernatural as the intellectual. Only with the coming of the Age of Reason was there any separation between areas of knowledge, such as astronomy and astrology.

Space

Space is intangible; we cannot pick it up and carry it somewhere else. We often imagine it to be a vast container, one that has no boundaries as it stretches into infinity. However, we still regard space as having some limit even though it is immeasurable. The concept of objects being some "distance" from each other is yet another idea that we cannot assume exists. Like time, space is an idealized abstraction.

The universe never breaks the laws of the conservation of energy. There is always "time symmetry" and "space symmetry"— an autonomous perfection. Surely, we may view the Grail in this way—it has a self-sufficiency that bestows form upon its essence. The field of vision that we use to view the Grail is narrowed and thus it acquires a greater intensity. The amount of conscious energy required to perceive the Grail somehow strengthens its very being.

In a state of ordinary consciousness, we encourage the brain to widen its conception of an idea in the belief that this will increase our understanding. This is in accord with John Locke's notion of *tabula rasa*—shaped by experience. In this philosophy, sensation and reflection are the sources of all ideas. The "association of ideas," as we have come to know it, encourages us to regard notions of similarity, continuity, and contrast as being aids to understanding. The medieval mind would not have comprehended such an approach, believing that only devotion was the key to understanding.

Space is composed entirely of atoms, all possessing incredible power and complexity and operating at speeds and spatial dimensions almost impossible to conceive. The brain is composed of about ten billion nerve cells, any one of which may connect with as many as 25,000 other nerve cells. The number of possible interconnections is far greater than all the atoms in the universe.

All this we term "spatial existence"—the "properties" of space being the myriads of atoms within it. What we term "spatial awareness" is regarding one object as being related to another in space. The other element of spatial existence is "substance." We may imagine anything we wish, but as soon as it becomes "substantial"—having "substance"—it exists independently of the imagination. Manifestation begins with an idea and, if successful, results in something that is independent of its original cause.

Thus, what we call "space" is the medium that permits objects to have an independent existence. If this was not so, nothing would have a material existence, and all would be qualitative rather than quantitative. One could have a very vivid idea of an object, but it could never be realised in three dimensions. Can we propose that the idea of the Grail is more real than any actuality? Does it always remain a vision and never become the actual object that the knights seek upon their Quest? Perhaps this accounts for the way that its ethereal presence haunts them—the Grail is somehow never quite close enough to grasp.

Space-Time

Space and time make up our experience of existence. Newtonian physics assumed that time was a constant. Noon GMT on Earth was the same anywhere in the universe. The concept of "space" or "here" and "there" was not taken into account. To pre-modern science, space and time were separate entities which had no effect upon each other. Einstein changed that mode of thinking when he proposed the concept of *space-time*, as Brian Greene explains.

> *"Space and time become players in the evolving cosmos. They come alive. Matter here causes space to warp there, which causes matter to move, which causes space way over there to warp even more, and so on. General relativity provides the choreography for an entwined cosmic dance of space, time, matter, and energy."*[37]

What happens if all objects are removed from space? Does space still exist? Is it then relegated to being just a location for the previously existing objects? Descartes and Leibnitz believed that space only existed as a framework. Its function was to demonstrate how objects were related to each other in terms of actual distance.

Einstein's Theory of Relativity suggested that objects could be extended in both space and time. Einstein was fortunate to have German mathematician Hermann Minkowski as a colleague who provided the key element to complete his theory. By including the dimension of time in the ordinary three dimensions of space, Minkowski conceived space-time. The Theory of Relativity is perhaps best understood with reference to Minkowski's thesis which was posited in 1909. As Minkowski predicted:

> *"Henceforth space by itself and time by itself are doomed to fade away into mere shadows and only a kind of union of the two will preserve its independent reality."*

Previously, time and space had been regarded as separate entities, each with its own nature and own exclusive rules. Now we conclude their nature is the same. Time is only a kind of space and infinite space is the same as eternity. In spiritual terms, this is expressed as the Buddha existing at the intersection of a number of different dimensions of being.

If time is only a kind of space, then infinite space is the same as eternity. If space is measured in three dimensions and time in another dimension, this gives a total of four. Time is often referred to as this "fourth dimension." This "space-time" gives us two points of reference, not only "where," but also "when." This appears to be a useful concept, as it is now possible to define more precisely when any event occurs. Any number of events may occupy the same point in space, one which stretches into infinity. Imagine each event as a person with arms outstretched, touching the fingertips of their neighbour. If we add the fourth dimension—time—then their existence in different places is possible. Like the Buddha, they will be "stretched" across time.

Because space-time is seen to be curved and represented as such, many space-time *continua* violate causality. When this happens, apparently paradoxical situations seem to exist—future events appear to affect the past. However, such an anomaly fits Arthur and the Grail perfectly. If one day Arthur will return and the Grail will be found, both these events may have already happened in the future. If this is so, then the passage of time between Arthur's journey to Avalon and the secreting of the Grail in Glastonbury by Joseph of Arimathea has a finite length. Arthur will return and the Grail will be found again; it is *fait accompli*.

Thus, with space-time, even if it is only a metaphysical concept, the philosopher has gained the advantage once more! Traditional science can never win in the game of speculation because it deals in assertions, which it attempts to verify. Those very assertions can only exist in a space-time framework.

In the Arthurian Tales is the ultimate example of a space-time event. It is that representation of the Golden Age and the place of our greatest dreams—Camelot. This acme of perfection was first depicted as a medieval dream city at the centre of Arthur's kingdom. In the Tales, Camelot is said to be downstream from Astolat, another fair city and the home of Elaine, of whom we have already spoken. The kingdom in which it is contained is said to be *Logres*, the old Welsh name for England. Camelot has been identified as being Cadbury Castle in Somerset, in South Cadbury village below Glastonbury.

The name Camelot may derive from *Camulus*, a Celtic god of war who the Romans identified with Mars, their own martial deity. Arthur, of Romano-Celtic stock, is a warrior king as well as a symbol of divinity, so the name "Camelot" may be apposite. The knights gather there, much jousting and sport take place, and many adventures are planned at the Round Table.

It is not only a place of pleasure but the symbol of the highest moral ideals. The Quest is announced there and thus the Grail contributes heavily to its ethos. This is the paradox of the Grail, the distance that it maintains from humanity. It may inspire piety but, incredibly, may not actually possess that quality. The Holy Vessel exists in a realm that is beyond ethical concerns; these are wholly the sphere of humanity.

Tennyson's *Idylls of the King* describes Camelot as being built to music. The poet hints at its other-worldly quality in the lines, "... *nothing in it is as it seems/Saving the King.*" This ability to occupy two states of existence at the same time is evinced by Arthur—*Rex Quondam, Rex Futurus*—one who vows to return and whose presence is never far away.

Another theory, relating to sub-atomic particles, is that matter going forward in time equals anti-matter going in the opposite direction. This adds even more credence to the possibility that objects may exist in the present, past, or future. We may not be able to see them, but there is no reason to suppose they are not actually there.

Faith is the key to the existence of King Arthur and the whole panoply of knights, fair maidens, sorcerers, and wizards. They once existed and there is no reason to suppose they do not continue to exist—and will always do so. Along with this is the belief that an extraordinary "something" that we choose to refer to as the Grail also exists. It may choose to remain hidden, but we may at any time be in touch with its presence—if only we have dedication enough to achieve this end.

VII. ALL IN PARALLEL

"OUR NORMAL WAKING CONSCIOUSNESS...IS
BUT ONE SPECIAL TYPE OF CONSCIOUSNESS,
WHILST ALL ABOUT IT, PARTED FROM IT BY
THE FILMIEST OF SCREENS, THERE LIES THE
POTENTIAL FORMS OF CONSCIOUSNESS ENTIRELY
DIFFERENT...NO ACCOUNT OF THE UNIVERSE IN
ITS TOTALITY CAN BE FINAL WHICH LEAVES
THESE OTHER FORMS OF CONSCIOUSNESS QUITE
DISREGARDED."

— WILLIAM JAMES

Any conception of the universe that accurately and completely reflects its singular nature is not easy to conceive. Previous notions, mainly based on Newtonian physics, have first to be discarded. Einstein wrote:

> "As far as the laws of mathematics refer to reality, they are not certain; and as far as they are certain, they do not refer to reality."[38]

The great man proposed that possibilities of "reality" could be described, but never reality itself. In quantum reality, it is accepted that any object has the ability to occupy two locations at the same time. Quantum physics proposes that we embrace all possibilities. Every event that has ever occurred since creation began exists somewhere in an alternative version. It does not matter that these have never been part of any actuality; they still have the potential to be.

Michio Kaku is a theoretical physicist and exponent of cosmology and succinctly provides our initial insight into quantum.

> *"...in a quantum play, the actors suddenly throw away the script and act on their own...The actors may disappear and reappear from the stage. Even stranger, they may find themselves appearing in two places at the same time."*[39]

Thus, we might conclude that the divine can be perceived simultaneously with the temporal. The mind must be the conduit of all spiritual experiences and so we conclude that the power of the universe resides within ourselves. We are the gods as well as the gods existing beyond us.

Quantum, the smallest particle known to scientists, has chaos at its centre. It seems we are constantly poised between order and anarchy. Like *The Fool* of the Tarot balancing on the cliff edge—will he jump or will he not? The problems of physics that quantum endeavours to solve are often answered in a manner that appears to refer more to metaphysics than science. In classical physics, a single object cannot be in two places at once, yet with quantum particles, the possibility is shown to exist. In a quantum system, the particle, when not being observed, can be in a multiplicity of places at once.

Consider how we might perceive the Grail, or King Arthur, if we had the good fortune to encounter either of them. Powerful entities project their own equally powerful aura, irrespective of their location in space and time. The images they produce exist indefinitely. Thus, we may "see" a great many extraordinary things or a version of the original transported to our consciousness.

This may account for the presence of ghosts and spirits that remain in a particular place for hundreds, or even thousands, of years. The Grail that was seen by the knights upon the Quest may resemble, in every detail, a vision of the Grail seen by a devout initiate in the twenty-first century. The treasure of Joseph of Arimathea may not be the same as the Grail seen by Sir Galahad. The Grail also increases in power the more it is revered, assuming an even greater beauty or wonder to those who behold it. Arthur also evokes this reaction by being seen to nurture and protect his people; they in turn fuel the inner strength he needs to achieve his royal—and we would say, his divine—purpose.

According to quantum theory, every object in the universe has a "wave function." This is not only its "presence" in one state, but its potential for existing in other states. By observing the object, we somehow determine the particular nature of the object. Before we make our observation, the object exists in all possible states— for instance, a tree might be standing upright or falling or a person might be alive or dead. In a parallel universe—as with quantum— there is every possible outcome.

Gotfried Leibniz, a proponent of Theodicy, proposed that *"God assuredly always chooses the best."*[40] Common sense tells us that we do not simultaneously perceive objects in all possible states. Neils Bohr concluded that once the object is perceived in its "definitive state," the wave function "collapses."

Every potential difference exists—we just don't see it. If the neurons in the brain behaved in a different way, it would be perfectly possible to see endless versions of the same event. We continue to perceive the object in the same way and the other possibilities simply cease to be. Broken eggs do not reassemble themselves. This is because the information pertaining to this happening is not preserved. It may be that for the purposes of our continuing evolution, some occurrences are simply not relevant.

The most well-known exemplar of this theory is known as "Schrodinger's Cat." It is an experiment that was never (thankfully) put into practice. A cat is sealed inside a box with a Geiger counter, a piece of uranium, and a flask of poison gas. If the device detects radiation through an atom of uranium happening to decay, the flask is automatically shattered. At any given moment, we do not know whether the cat is alive or dead. Quantum mechanics suggests that the cat is simultaneously in both states—they are co-existent. Yet when we look into the box, we expect to see the cat either alive or dead, not both.

Schrodinger's proposal cannot be dismissed as a pointless paradox or an affront to any method of logical thinking. It is a succinct demonstration that uncertainty is as intrinsic to the universe as any other factor. Not everyone has been impressed by this view, Einstein famously remarking *"God does not play dice with the world."* Bohr's riposte, less often quoted, was, *"Stop telling God what to do!"*

Goldilocks Zone

In trillions of years, a dead, dark universe will have taken the place of the one we know now. As Joseph Campbell tells us:

> *"The basic principle of all mythology is this of the beginning in the end. Creation myths are pervaded with a sense of the doom that is continually recalling all created shapes to the imperishable out of which they first emerged."*[41]

In every era, the current generation tends to assume that the time they live in is the most enlightened or progressive. There is a tendency to assume that the universe we live in is the absolute version, this evolution being progressive and logical. But as Hume remarked:

> *"Numerous universes might have been botched and bungled throughout an eternity, ere this system was struck out; much labour lost, many fruitless trials made, and a slow but continual improvement carried out during infinite ages in the art of world-making."*

This brings into play the notion of the "goldilocks zone," the idea that the Earth exists because its situation is perfectly suited to the point it occupies in the universe. Our planet is situated precisely the correct distance from the Sun to maintain life, and this is not the only fortuitous occurrence. Consider, besides Earth, Europa (one of the moons of Jupiter) is the only body in our galaxy that has water on its surface. Without water, life could not survive on the planet. We are indeed fortunate—or, looking at it another way, perhaps we selected our own particular universe because it was the most suitable for us.

This is the anthropic principle one where biological factors constrain the universe to be in a "perfect" state to maintain life upon the Earth. If its age were any younger or older, conditions would not be conducive to the planet's existence. That is not to say that alternative versions of Earth do not exist—it is likely that they do, as we are about to discover.

Parallel Universes

Concerning the concept of a "parallel universe" we cannot better this account by Fred Alan Wolf:

> *"Like an everyday universe it is a region of space and time containing matter, galaxies, stars, planets and living beings. In other words, a parallel universe is similar and possibly even a duplicate of our own universe. Not only in a parallel universe must there be other human beings, but these may be human beings who are exact duplicates of ourselves and who are connected to ourselves through mechanisms only explainable using quantum physics concepts."[42]*

Wolf also maintains, as do other quantum physicists, that entry to a parallel universe must be through a "black hole." This is implied because black holes distort the space-time surrounding them. Yet, far from being an aberration, a black hole is simply another topological feature in space.

Parallel universes may have an existence that is so close to us that the gap between them is almost negligible. They may be in a higher dimension of space—super space. States of mind that we are aware of but do not entirely understand—lucid dreaming, astral travel, even schizophrenia—they too may exist here. Less than the thickness of an atom may separate us from the Grail, our goal...but it is enough. The esoteric expression "Beyond the Veil" begins to take on a whole new meaning.

Perhaps the actual concept of a "universe" is redundant, and we should consider a "multiverse" as being a more plausible explanation. If the various stages in the process of evolution are, as it were, connected to each other by trapdoors or tunnels in time, the world we inhabit may simply be one of many. The Earth is simply one of a number of existences, all in an endless procession from the past into the future, and all existing at the same moment of time.

Consciousness

Another "wolf," Virginia *Woolf,* had this to say concerning the mind, the way that it:

> *"...receives myriad impressions—trivial, fantastic, evanescent, or engraved with the sharpness of steel. From all sides they come, an incessant shower of innumerable atoms...life is a luminous halo, a semi-transparent envelope surrounding us from the beginning of consciousness to the end."[43]*

Defining "consciousness" is the greatest challenge to any understanding of how we perceive the universe. Why is the causation of behaviour accompanied by a conscious inner life? How does the brain integrate information? Is the state of consciousness simply an ocean of events that flood the brain?

What decides how a particular stimulus commands our attention at any particular time is a matter for conjecture. Is the process of selecting a particular thought entirely random? Or does one chunk of data assert itself above its neighbours and, at a given moment, occupy our entire focus?

We are rarely aware of a state of "consciousness" or even being "conscious" except in a very mundane manner. A statement such as "I'm feeling cold" exhibits an aspect of consciousness, but the information volunteered by the individual may be unreliable or incorrect. The assessment of such a state—awareness of experiencing a low temperature—may be plausible *at that moment* but is not necessarily accurate for any duration of time.

Conventional science is tempted to dismiss the whole notion of consciousness as being an "illusion." If consciousness is a "natural" phenomenon, then its nature will be determined by natural laws. These may differ from any "physical" laws. Daniel Dennet informs us that:

> *"Human consciousness...can best be understood as the operation of a...virtual machine implemented in the parallel architecture of a brain that was not designed for such activities. The powers of this virtual machine vastly enhance the underlying powers of the organic hardware on which it runs."[44]*

Psychology teaches us that consciousness begins in the unconscious mind. All our perceptions originate there, reflected upon first before they are eventually made manifest. Descartes memorably wrote, *"I realise that I should not be surprised at God's doing things that I can't explain."* In his seminal work *The Meditations* he proposed that in our search for the truth, we should first doubt our own perceptions.

We are only ever given a hint of the truth, and we can never own a monopoly on absolute reality. In recent decades, science has grown closer to philosophy in that much thinking and research now belong in the realm of metaphysics. Some are hostile to any transcendental aspect and remove themselves as far away as possible from such debate. Tomberg details this outworn approach in the following way:

> *"... the scientific ideal is to reduce the multiplicity of phenomena to a limited number of laws and then reduce these to a single simple formula. It is a mater, in the last analysis, of mechanising the intellect in such manner that it calculates the world instead of understanding it."[45]*

He widens the thesis by comparing the principles of magick to:

"... *Hermeticism [which] is contrary to that of science. Instead of aspiring to own power over the forces of Nature by means of the destruction of matter, Hermeticism aspires to conscious participation with the constructive forces of the world on the basis of an alliance and a cordial communion with them.*"[46]

Has it been forgotten that "science" has its origins in magick, or "natural philosophy" as it was once titled?

Our own individual consciousness makes us who we are. Testing and expanding our view of the world helps us to develop our knowledge and understanding. "Consciousness" is simply a term we use to describe the experience of "awareness" generated by the cells of the brain. If "quantum reality" has a monopoly on how everything is perceived, then we are only able to experience that. We assume that every individual has the choice as to how they perceive anything, but this may not be the case. The nature and number of those choices may be determined by reality itself.

Much has been made of the phenomena that had occurred in the few years that led up to 2012, a date of great significance to many. It is said that the Earth's magnetic field, the barrier that protects us from solar wind, had shifted its rotation at this time. This invisible area in space is three and half billion years old. It projects tens of thousands of miles into space out from the Earth and often appears to act quite unpredictably.

The appearance of crop circles, the sighting of UFOs, and the increased incidence of schizophrenia were all cited as evidence of Jung's thesis that we were approaching a time when "the dream becomes real." It may be that individual psychic skills would have returned to the level of sensitivity that they owned thousands of years ago. Then there was no conscious division between the spiritual and the secular "consciousness." The reference to schizophrenia is more than because in the original Greek, the word meant "broken soul" or "broken heart." It is as if a "global healing" was needed, and quantum would have been the catalyst.

If, as many considered possible, there were to be a "Quantum Awakening" the description of this moment has dramatic overtones, as Ken Carey explained:

> *"In this moment the smallest interval of time—the interval that occurs in every atom between each of its billions of oscillations per second—will be lengthened unto infinity. An interval of neo-time will expand. Through that expansion eternity will flow. Some will experience this moment as minutes or hours, others as a lifetime. Still others will experience this flash of non-time as a succession of many lives..."*[47]

Changing Reality

Do we possess the powers to alter the nature of reality? Can this be achieved simply by changing the way we regard our own existence? If our conception of the world is based upon our experiences of it, then should we not be able to apply that information in a different way? The nature of a quantum state is that it always has the potential for change. Perhaps this dictum may be applied to our consciousness. We may not be able to make any state of reality cease to exist, but it may be possible to substitute that reality for another. This may happen when a second reality becomes the centre of our focus.

Merlin, the celebrated wizard in the Arthurian tales, has much to contribute to our understanding of the Grail. He is not its custodian, but he does inaugurate the Quest, and by doing so, personifies the magickal characteristics of the Grail. Merlin is elusive, "the trickster" of the Shamanic tradition. Like any magician, he knows how to occupy the space between the worlds. Thus, he is in exactly the right place to evoke the Grail, for within the Inner Planes is where its essence may be found.

Discovering the whereabouts of our own sacred centre does not occur within any chronological period of time; it is the culmination of experience gained during our own quest. It is as if there are two parallel existences during any life, one experienced day by day, the other eternal, not defined by time. If we had constant access to this other existence, we could be able to "see" without reference to everyday reality. We will then subscribe to the Buddhist teaching of being "in the world but not of the world."

Many Dimensions

Physicists do not agree on the number of possible dimensions there may be. To qualify as a separate dimension, this "mini-universe" must be entirely different from its neighbour. If we regard these as time streams, can events on one be detected from another? If so, this may provide an explanation for a phenomenon such as *déjà-vu*—an unconscious glimpse of a previous life, one running concurrently with a present incarnation.

The knight upon the Quest could pass from one dimension of time into another, and there discover the Grail. Our hero would have to make sure he returned to the exact point where he had made the crossover between dimensions! If the structure of such time streams were to branch or loop, it would be possible to connect with events in the past or the future. Might one time stream be somehow more prominent than another? We might choose a particular life because our instinct tells us to do so.

"Change" and "time" are not synonymous. We may observe the budding of a leaf in spring and its withering in the autumn and conclude that this illustrates the passing of time. The two moments are not necessarily connected, however, we only assume that this is so. The months between the two events may be counted, but all measuring of time is arbitrary. We cannot describe the passing of an hour with any certainty.

Universal Consciousness

Matter is always in motion—always changing. The universe is expanding every nanosecond. The hundred billion galaxies that exist will have already increased in the time it takes to read these words. The expansion is not capable of being observed; there is just "more space available" at particular times. The universe is measurable and yet infinite at the same time. Cosmologists name this paradox the "cosmological constant."

We associate the "light" of the Grail with "realisation." By doing this, we are in accord with a fundamental principle of physics in that any exchange of energy between two atoms involves photons. Thus, light penetrates the entire universe and also connects every part. We may say that material light and the light of consciousness, which are indivisible, lie somewhere beyond time and space.

It seems likely that the synapses in the brain function in a manner very similar to "quantum randomness." The "method" of certain aspects of consciousness may simply be unknown. It is pertinent that random number generators may be affected by the human brain. Also, if a significant number of people are affected by a traumatic event, then "common perception" is affected. A study made in 2002 of the effects of the September 11 terrorist attacks in America on number generators confirmed this theory. This excerpt from the research conducted at Princeton University is remarkable:

> *"... the September 11 results imply that there is a correlation between the intensity or impact of an event and the strength of deviations in the data. The September 11 event is arguably the most extreme in the database in terms of its social, psychological, emotional, and global impact. As the analysis has shown, it also exhibits the largest and most consistent deviations in the database on the statistical measures we have investigated."[48]*

Another equally diverting study is in the field of parapsychology—specifically psychokinesis. This is the ability of any person to predict with certainty the outcome of a series of random events. Research in this area was initially conducted with Zener cards—a series of five different symbols, each one printed on an individual card. The subject must predict which of the five will appear when the card is turned over. Karl Zener, the originator of the system, found the results to have been of interest but largely inconsequential. The success rate was too random to form a basis for any conclusion.

J.B. Rhine, Zener's colleague in the 1930s, devised a more interesting study. He had constructed a machine that randomly rolled six dice. Those in the study group attempted to determine which numbers appeared. Rhine effectively demonstrated that with the same participant observing the roll thousands of times, he could eventually affect the outcome. This is truly "mind over matter."

We may enquire if a change in consciousness affects quantum or vice versa? Certainly, "intuitive" thinking may reveal a perspective that had not appeared to exist previously. The clairvoyant is "one step ahead" of the majority who appear to have little or no psychic ability. The "psychic" trusts in the "meaning" of what they "see." Can we conclude that it is this "awareness" that creates a universe of infinite meaning? The astronomer Sir James Jeans wrote in 1932:

> *"Mind no longer appears as an accidental intruder into the realm of matter; we are beginning to suspect that we ought rather to hail it as the creator and governor of the realm of matter..."*[49]

We realize that there is a difference between what we are capable of seeing and what is actually there. Quantum demonstrates that matter is "fuzzy clouds of potential existence," very far from the "solid state" that we so fondly believe it is. Our "thinking" cannot claim to have any substance and apparently neither does the world!

In the Eastern tradition, the state of *samadhi* is the "still mind"— the ultimate goal of meditation. A different kind of consciousness from waking, dreaming, or sleep, awareness is present, but thoughts or images do not modify the state. We can only claim that *samadhi* is yet another version of reality, not the ultimate.

The Unknown

We live in a phenomenal rather than a causal universe and material changes are unpredictable. Physical objects exist because they have a function of "self-identity." An object does not capriciously take on the form of another, although the shamanic practice of shapeshifting indicates the illusion is possible to maintain. At this point, physics and magick diverge, as traditional science does not acknowledge the shaman's skills as anything other than a talent for deception.

The delightfully titled "New Mysterianism," a principle advocated by Noam Chomsky among others, proposes that being totally familiar with the workings of the universe is an achievement beyond even the most powerful intellect.[50] No amount of computation or research can result in constructing a blueprint of creation. The assumption that it is within the capability of man to comprehend all nature is regarded as absurd by the New Mysterians. Is it possible to share completely or accurately any view rising from the subjective consciousness?

Kant spoke of *ding an sich*— "the thing in itself," independent of any subjective perception. Objective reality insists that if a situation exists in a particular mode, then that is what is happening. As we have discovered, this is an illusion, and our subjective reality is also quite capable of creating illusions. In effect, we can only define anything objectively by a consensual agreement as to its nature—and so we return to the dubious practice of conventional thinking!

But does all this simply leave us in a state of universal doubt? Do we feel abandoned in a place where, having nothing to hold onto, we feel uncomfortable? Yet, the opposite should be true; despite all our insecurities, we should have arrived at a plateau of understanding. The place of all things in the universe is assured and we interact with every other being, creature, and living thing upon the planet. All things are interconnected, and this realization, like beholding the Grail, should give us the greatest joy.

The Wise Fool

Panpsychism maintains that all matter is sentient and part of a universal consciousness. A universe where every detail is predictable, conforming to some kind of inevitable logic, would be ineffably tedious. Creation counters this by making every part of the universe unique. Even two blades of grass are not identical, and every human on the planet has their own idiosyncrasies.

We may cite a mathematical example to demonstrate our thesis. The distribution of prime numbers appears to be unpredictable, and yet there are mathematicians who believe a formula exists to dispute this—it is just a matter of discovering it. Mathematician Don Zagier came to this almost paradoxical conclusion:

> *"... despite their simple definition and role as the building blocks of the natural numbers, the prime numbers grow like weeds among the natural numbers, seeming to obey no other law than chance, and nobody can predict where the next one will sprout...even more astonishing the prime numbers exhibit stunning regularity, that there are laws governing their behaviour, and that they obey these laws with almost military precision."[51]*

As soon as we attempt to set out an ultimate definition of anything, nature has a habit of conspiring against us. *Enantiodromia* is an ancient Greek term that refers to the tendency of any phenomenon to reverse itself. Without any prior warning, it does a backflip. To create a world which is devoid of logic yet has within it some undeniable sense of order leans towards the domain of art, particularly literature.

Lewis Carroll was a lecturer in Mathematics at Oxford, an academic with a formidable intellect. With equal diligence, he used his cerebral powers to create the topsy-turvy world of *Alice in Wonderland* and *Alice through the Looking Glass*. Martin Gardner was editor of *The Annotated Alice* and a Carroll scholar. With reference to *Wonderland,* he provides an interesting insight into reason's eternal struggle with unreason.

"At the heart of things science finds only a mad, never-ending quadrille of Mock Turtle Waves and Gryphon Particles. For a moment the waves and particles dance in grotesque, inconceivably complex patterns capable of reflecting on their own absurdity."[52]

The indeterminate, shifting nature of our world has always attracted the artist and the thinker. Fascinated by ambiguity and oblique ways of seeing the world, this very uncertainty in creation is regarded by creative people as one of its greatest virtues. The multi-faceted crystal that is existence shines brighter when wit and jest are reflected in it. The essence of humour is the "hidden variable," the spontaneous reaction. All are part of "reality" and life would be much the poorer without laughter and joy.

We should offer our deepest gratitude that we have been given the ability to mock ourselves when we take life too seriously. Humour is the ultimate detachment, and as such, has the highest spiritual goals. It has no ties to the material world and never wishes for any. There is more profundity in a *bon mot* such as, "the universe is God's joke—one that no one ever gets," than in many volumes of theology.

Alfred Jarry was a pioneer of the "Theatre of the Absurd," a movement in the France of the 1900s. *Ubu Roi* was his most renowned and controversial play, but he was also remembered for conceiving the notion of "pataphysics." Jarry himself described this "science" as *extending as far beyond metaphysics as the latter extends beyond physics.* It was to be a study based *on the truth of contradictions and exceptions.* It was also:

"...the science of imaginary solutions, which symbolically attributes the properties of objects, described by their virtuality, to their lineaments."[53]

Such a statement is delightfully ridiculous. No matter how deeply the words are reflected upon, the reader always returns to the text none the wiser. This is what is so delightful about Jarry's "absurdist" writings; they appear at first glance to be plausible explanations of physics or gems of philosophy. *"God equals the tangential point between zero and infinity"* is a sublime example.

Writers who become too involved in the profundity of their own theories should regularly refer to the following. It will serve as a palliative.

> *"If you let a coin fall and it falls, the next time it is just by an infinite coincidence that it will fall again the same way; hundreds of other coins on other hands will follow this pattern in an infinitely unimaginable fashion."*[54]

Jarry's comic masterpiece was *How to Construct a Time Machine*. Any part of the work may be quoted, but perhaps the opening sentence best demonstrates the flavour of the piece:

> *"A Time Machine, that is, a device for exploring Time, is no more difficult to conceive of than a Space Machine, whether you consider Time as the fourth dimension of Space or as a locus essentially different because of its contents."*

The revival of an interest in the Grail is indicative of a change in the zeitgeist. Perhaps the holy vessel is a symbol of the transformation that will occur when the human mind and body are eventually linked. Individual consciousness will have no separate existence from anything else in the universe. The complexity of this kind of transformation hints at a process that is beyond natural evolution. Changes in man's growth invariably occur at a fitful rate indicating that other forces—cognitive and intuitive—are the *deus ex machina* of human development.

The remarks of Max Planck summarise our conclusion:

> *"Science cannot solve the ultimate mystery of Nature. And it is because in the last analysis we ourselves are part of the mystery we are trying to solve."*[55]

VIII. MOON MAIDEN

"... I GUINEVERE
MADE MY QUEEN'S EYES SO GRACIOUS AND MY
HAIR
DELICATE WITH GOLD IN ITS SOFT WAYS
AND MY MOUTH HONIED SO FOR LANCELOT."

— SWINBURNE

A male symbol may be the tower, pillar, or minaret—the female; the door, the ship, or the ring. That the Grail is a depiction of the essence of femininity seems self-evident. In ancient cultures, masculine and feminine attributes were often depicted in a graphic manner. The *lingam* and the *yoni* are, respectively, the male and female emblems in Sanskrit. The *sistrum* was a percussion instrument used in the worship of Isis and represents, by the horizontal bars across the *fenestrum*, the *virgo intacta*.

The Queen of Heaven is also the Celestial Mother and a virgin, if we are able to embrace such an apparently contradictory concept! The medieval consciousness considered virginity to be akin to innocence rather than simply a physical state. The purity of the untarnished Earth, the fecundity and budding fertility that follows is the great miracle of the Goddess. She awaits her consort as Aphrodite awaits her lover, Ares. After her willing surrender, she waits patiently to give birth to her child, bringing life once more to the universe in a never-ending cycle.

The explicitness of Hindu temple carvings shocked the Victorians who travelled in India, but these images actually embody holiness. The prudes, who condemned such depictions of conjugal bliss, convinced themselves that the act of love was somehow separate from affection. Our ancestors knew the true power of sex, incorporating it as the union of god and goddess into their magickal ceremonies. In the Qabalistic Tree of Life, Yesod is named "The Hidden Valley." This Sephira has dominion over the genitals, that part of the physical body from where all magick springs.

The Goddess forever tests us, particularly our faith in the rightness of things. Her love is unconditional, and the Goddess expects us to be the same with her. If we are to be truly one with her, we must accept *all* her ways—from the terrible to the sublime. She is the mirror of the lake as well as the fathomless seas. Her love is endless and eternal as are all her passions.

In the Celtic tradition, every goddess has, as her basic nature, that of an Earth goddess—Epona and Rhiannon being the most celebrated. Each of the female figures in the Arthurian Tales represents some aspect of the Goddess. The tri-partite aspect of the lunar goddess—the virgin, bride, and crone—gives us a starting point in our deliberations.

Avalon

Avalon is the faery realm, situated in the West and the spiritual heart of England, the centre of Albion. It is the Promised Land, the Realm of Perfection, this Holiest Earth, and Isle of the Blest—*Insula Pomerium* or *Ynis Witrin* (the Island of Apples or the Island of Glass). One Celtic legend depicts the place as a revolving glass island with four horns—a land of the dead and of ghosts. It is also similar to the Fortunate Isles of the Greeks and also to Elysium.

One school of Arthurian lore suggests with much conviction, but less evidence, that Wales is the landscape of Arthur. Others champion Scotland or Cornwall, and yet another school insists upon Brittany as being the location of Avalon. Being of a transcendental nature, the Arthurian tales cannot be aligned to any precise time or space. For the purposes of our study, we will consider the Isle of Avalon to be in the moorlands of Somerset.[56] Glastonbury has always been considered the place where the Grail was hidden by Joseph of Arimathea, and Avalon is traditionally sustained by the holy vessel.

The association of Avalon with apples suggests that this particular fruit has the power to open up a world of enchantment. Cider is made from apples, and that intoxicating brew is capable of producing a certain otherworldly state! It is said that a certain kind of crab apple has hallucinogenic properties. Was the imbibing of these psychedelic fruits a means of obtaining mystic visions—some evoking the paradise of Avalon?

Hercules stole the secret of immortality from the serpent Ladon, and apples are often used to symbolize ambrosia, the food of the gods. Avalon may only exist in the mind, perhaps making it even more enticing as a land of faery.[57] Is it the world of the imagination alone that can sustain it? Perhaps if exposed to the vibrations of an unsympathetic, material world, this sacred kingdom simply disappears.

Goddess of Light

Guinevere, being the consort of Arthur, represents the earthly part of his power—the actual kingdom. In the Welsh tradition, she is *Blodwenn*—the "flower bride" whose physical form is made entirely of flowers. Guinevere is also Queen of the May, her festival being *Beltane* on the first day of that month. Like *The Empress* of the Tarot, Guinevere has a crown of stars about her; she is Venus/Aphrodite. Her essential goodness assigns her the title, like Isis, of "the Queen of Heaven." Guinevere symbolizes the eternal, sympathetic relationship between the potency of the king and the fertility of the land, a tradition supported by the ancient Irish texts. These hint that a king might be ritually married to the tutelary Earth goddess of the tribe.

Guinevere does not possess supernatural powers, but she has all the attributes of a great queen, having a rare beauty and great gifts of intellect and conversation. She is also highly sensual, yearning to be possessed—and here lies the tragedy, for she can never be satisfied with such a disinterested lover as Arthur. Despite Merlin's magickal machinations to continue the line of the Royal Blood, the Grail will not be gained, and Logres will forever remain enchanted and unredeemed. Thus, the unloved Guinevere seeks the consoling arms of Lancelot. It is an act that will guarantee the fall of the kingdom.

In some traditions, Nimue (the Lady of the Lake) and Morgan le Fay blend into one composite figure. In the Tarot they are, respectively, the Arcana of *The High Priestess* and *Death*. They are both aspects of Isis and she is the Moon, inexorably linked to romance. When Cupid comes upon us when least expected, we fall, often madly, in love. Shared past lives may be responsible for bringing together a particular man and woman. How lovers radiate the light of love! Theirs is a world of sweet words and soft caresses—the closeness of perfumes and incense—a world of intimacy. Yet a commitment to each other must eventually be made, or all is merely froth and fantasy—moonbeams.

Lucius Apuleius, the Roman poet, describes the Goddess as wearing a green robe of nature decorated with flowers and fruits as well as possessing a black robe, signifying the inevitability of death. Another vision of her, from Apuleius, is particularly evocative:

> *"A boat-shaped dish of gold hung from her left hand and along the surface of the handle writhed an asp with a puffed throat and head raised ready to strike."*[58]

When Arthur falls in battle, the wounded king insists he will go to Avalon to the kingdom ruled by Argante, the Queen of the Elves, and be healed. This queen has many other names—*Argel* (silver swan), *Airgid Roth* (silver wheel), *Eirianwen* (silver white), *Arianeira* (silver snow), and *Pressina* (the nine-fold goddess). She is a Moon goddess who descended into the sea and who also has a stone circle dedicated to her.

Argante is seated upon a throne of crystal; she is tall and slender with sea green eyes, long red-gold hair, and white skin. She has an affinity with Guinevere (The White One), and Ygraine, the mother of Arthur and Raghnell (White Raven), Queen of the Wastelands. The willow is sacred to her as it always grows beside water.

Goddess of Darkness

Morgan le Fay, however, is destined to lead Arthur into the otherworld. It is she who is the Queen of Faery and also the figure of Death. Does Death have a distinct sex? In his fantasy novels, Terry Pratchett portrays Death, most convincingly, as a male figure. Morgan resembles a Norse Valkyrie, one who takes the souls of dead warriors to Valhalla. It is difficult to imagine the Queen of the Underworld in any other way.

In her barque the "Coracle of Cerridwen," Morgan will take Arthur to Avalon. The parent of Morgan le Fay was Modron—"The Great Mother"—reputedly a priestess of Isis. Morgan appears as a mother archetype, and as the Great Mother, may act in a cruel or kind manner. This is the nature of Morgan le Fay—she is both. Morgan ferries the dead to the underworld herself, giving her an affinity with Persephone, the Queen of Hades, or even Hecate. Like that dark deity, Morgan is certainly capable of casting spells to exact revenge.

She may also be *Morgawse*, and in this incarnation, she embodies the characteristics of Scorpio. In its manifestation as the Eagle and the Snake, Scorpio embraces both the elements of Air and Earth, while still retaining the essence of that most elusive element—Water. And so alone with Morgan le Fay, or in another version, accompanied by two other queens who mourn him (Guinevere and Vivienne—the Lady of the Lake), Arthur drifts slowly to Avalon and his end. Morgan le Fay rules this land, although some texts fleetingly mention two figures with pretensions to that throne—Avalloch and Guinguemar.

Depicted as an enchantress in the Arthurian tales, Morgan personifies man's fear of all that which he fervently desires. The male anxiety is that, when confronted by such an enchantress, he will lose control of the situation and become a slave to his passions. Neither is the enchantress also without a dangerous ambivalence. She wishes to destroy the hero or keep him prisoner in her own realm.

This encounter with the *femme fatale* is one of the perils in which the true hero must experience and survive in order to continue upon his journey. Morgan is also Hecate, who Zeus honoured above every other goddess and gave her dazzling gifts; a share of the Earth, and a share of the barren sea. It is the nature of the enchantress to fascinate and to be alluring. Those who fall under her spell discover just how wayward she may be. Her moods rise and fall as do the tides, and she is quite capable of being as cruel as the endless oceans. Like Circe, she is cold and ruthless and leads men to their doom without a qualm.

Morgan le Fay owns all wisdom and knowledge, within her heart are all memories and all deeds. She is all-seeing, and through her sorcery, able to assume any appearance—the heart's desire of any man. She could have been a mighty warrior queen, but she chose to be a sorceress. As the dark side of Mars, she is all the more deadly if challenged. It is the role of the Goddess to accept all, she forgives us again and again—we are all her children.

She should be worshipped at those times of the year when the seasons change from warmth to coolness—at *Samhain* when the veil between the worlds is so very thin. The Goddess will always be our guide in the darkness. She knows too where she may find the light—it is within her, the light of the changing, motherly Moon.

Man and Maiden

Morgan may be *Pressina*, sometimes known as the "nine-fold goddess." This half-woman, half-fish is from another world, as there is much of the Otherworld in Morgan le Fay. She has "Nine Maidens of the Grail" attending her in Avalon. That Morgan is a renowned healer is never in question, and her nine followers, either her daughters or sisters, are skilled in the art as well.

The Gnostic faith stressed that men and women alike may be "priest or prophet." Sophia, the female complement of Christ, represents the healing aspect needed by the wounded king. This is the Gnostic sense of the "spirit"—Fortuna or the Black Madonna. In magickal symbolism, Fire and Water (two intertwined triangles respectively pointing upward and downward) are combined to form the Star of David, a symbol of the meeting of the higher and lower natures.

In the Chinese tradition, Heaven (Yang) is formed first and Earth (Yin) at a later time. According to Chinese tradition, the union of the Sun (Yang) and the Moon (Yin) produced the stars and planets. This is the divine meeting of male and female, and in ancient Egypt and Mesopotamia, creation was regarded as a shared responsibility—one of god and goddess. This combination of Fire and Water is said to manifest The Holy Spirit.

To make Arthur whole, he needs the Grail—the female soul. His *animus* must be united with the *anima*. It is as if both Arthur and the Grail must emerge from their hiding place and their subsequent union be revealed to the world. Thus, Arthur the warrior god is laid to rest to fight no more—at least not in this lifetime. As the prince wakes the sleeping princess with a kiss, in a reversal of roles, Isis will restore life to her consort, for Arthur is Osiris, the sacrificial king.

Once and Future King

Folk tales have always indicated that there are heroes who are preserved in a kind of limbo, ready to reappear and rescue a threatened nation should the need arise. King Arthur is undoubtedly the most well-known example of such a cult—if it can be so described. Other figures, although less well-known, are equally well-documented.

King Wenzel lies sleeping under the Blanik Mountains in Bohemia. He, it is said, will return to Prague and the people will take up once more the sword of Bruncvik to defeat the enemies of his country. Frederick Barbarossa lives, reputedly, beneath a mountain in Thuringia, and when "the ravens cease to fly" he will return and restore his country to its greatness. Ogier the Dane, once the enemy of Charlemagne but later his ally in a campaign against the Saracens, will supposedly return to rescue Denmark in times of danger. This great leader is supposed to have lived in Avalon for two hundred years, so it is not only Arthur who enjoys the privilege of residing in the sacred kingdom.

Avalon is a place where time does not exist. Being a mortal, Arthur must remain there if he wishes to preserve his life. In other versions, he will eventually be healed, but the time that must elapse for this to happen appears to be endless. So here is reputedly the resting place of *Rex Quondam, Rex Futurus.*

The ambiance of the Isle of Avalon is unique for the reason that the Old and the New faiths are there balancing each other. With the demise of Christianity at the end of the Age of Pisces, the Age of Aquarius is at last making its mark. The New Age does not seek to stamp out Christianity—or it should not do so if it is to remain true to its ideals.

Before its destruction at the time of the Reformation, Glaston-bury Abbey was a magnificent example of twelfth-century Gothic architecture. Enough of its fabric remains to give the visitor some conception of its former grandeur. The monks possessed an impressive collection of relics pertaining to Christ's Passion. The hoard was extensive and includes parts of the table from the Last Supper, pieces of the Cross, a spike from the Crown of Thorns, and some fragments of the Holy Sepulcher. Having the Grail would have been the crowning glory for the monks, and as we have learned in the tale of the Nanteos Cup, this may well have been so.

Wisdom of Women

The Word (*Logos*) must always be linked with Wisdom (*Sophia*). Sophia is the mediator, the interpreter of the Divine Will—a role which she fills to perfection. Sophia is "The Voice of the Wells," a beloved theme of the medieval troubadours and represents the wisdom of the Grail. The Philosopher's Stone is the alchemical term for this wisdom and is often known as the Sophistical Stone.

The essence of both "Marys"—The Virgin Mary and Mary Magdalene—is to be found within the character of Sophia. She attempts to reconcile what has been seen for too long as an irredeemable conflict. Sophia embraces the spiritual and the material. Mary the Virgin was only grudgingly accepted by the

Church of England, while Mary Magdalene is the *bête-noir* of both the Catholic and the Protestant faiths. Wrongly castigated by the Church Fathers whose prejudice was only exceeded by their ignorance; Mary Magdalene has finally emerged for her true worth. She is the Bride of Christ. It is within the Grail and behind the veil of Isis that such great secrets have been preserved for so long.

Isis reveals herself only to a few, and when those chosen are in her presence, they are aware that they stand before the Divine Goddess. It is no wonder that the profane are denied this honour, for even the devout must be of stout heart and unshakeable faith to withstand such an experience. Isis causes the manifestation of the material from out of the astral realms. All is in her image; all that can be seen upon the material plane is but the vision of the Goddess. The munificence—the eternal wisdom of the Goddess— is in all things.

Isis was schooled by Thoth, the god of wisdom and writing. From him, she learned much wisdom. He is a god who, although associated with the underworld, predominantly represents the element of Air—ideas and communication. In the Tarot, Air is assigned to the suit of Swords. Here we have a variation of the Lance/Grail pairing; this is the union of Sword/Grail, the fusion between the intellect and the spirit. Hermes or Mercury is the hero who "fertilizes the vase."

The hilt of a magickal sword must be of copper (the metal governed by Venus) so that it balances the iron of Mars. This is yet another meeting of god and goddess, and without such a union, the sword is worthless as a magickal artefact. A sword made solely of steel has only the will to guide it, and thus may be used for good or ill.

As with Jupiter, Venus is regarded by astrologers as being a beneficent planet. At her highest vibration she radiates goodness and beauty and so has the power to be transmuted into the sword of truth, for as the poet would have us believe, "beauty is truth."

Seekers of the Sixties

Towards the end of the 1960s, a desire to discover where the mystical path would lead took hold of a generation. In Britain, a few had dabbled with Eastern philosophy, but it was their own rich heritage that would eventually capture their hearts. Their yearning to explore was more than satisfied, for the British Isles has beyond its fair share of myth and legend—enough to occupy anyone for a lifetime, if not several.

Many a young man of those times resembled himself a figure from Arthurian legend. He sported shoulder length hair, a beard, and had a long velvet cloak draped about his shoulders. Many of them had been taught history in the boarding schools of the 1950s and this ensured a foundation for their studies. Suffer a harsh regime at the hands of their *alma mater* they did, but their souls were tempered by the experience and more than ready for any journey into the unknown.

Professing many a different vision, a coterie of artists, writers, poets, and musicians, spiced with a sprinkling of the English aristocracy, converged on the quiet Somerset town of Glastonbury on most weekends. Some were the elite of fashionable London; others had abandoned their moneyed roots for a rural idyll, albeit temporary. There was much to attract those who wanted to be part of the scene. It was a heady mix of philosophy, mysticism, and the exotic. Together with the added allure of the company of pop stars and a few drop-out intellectuals, it was all very irresistible.

These gatherings of scholars and young idealists who were determined to change the world, by peaceful and conscious-changing means, had all the romance of the age of Hazlitt and Lamb. At the foot of the Tor, views were expounded around a campfire, deliberations continuing into the early hours. These were the golden times, a few years before the Pilton music festival put Avalon on the map, and the face of Glastonbury was to be changed forever.

There were certainly a few raised eyebrows in the town. At that time, conservative residents were not used to the sight of troubadours, sages, and fairy queens processing along the streets. However, there was no overt hostility; confrontation was not the political or social issue that it was to become in the following decades. These seekers of the 60s were affable, gentle idealists, the cream of hippiedom—the beautiful people. Tolkien and folk songs inspired them—they lived in a world of sunshine, moonlit reflections, and sweet reverie.

A particular group of devotees was attracted to Glastonbury not only for the associations of the Isle of Avalon, but as part of a blossoming interest in UFOs. Though it might now seem extraordinary, the possibility of flying saucers landing on top of the Tor was considered to be not only possible, but likely.

Is the UFO phenomenon something outside our own conceptions of time and space? In the 1950s, Jung was of the view that "things seen in the sky" were portents of a transformation of the collective psyche. There has always been a fascination for the idea that we were not the only form of life in the galaxies, and logic informs us that it is highly unlikely that we are. The next question is, if we are not alone, what form do our galactic neighbours take? Even if they do communicate with us, can we understand their language? If another civilization is communicating with our Earth, does this indicate that they do not have the ability to travel into our galaxy?

The notion that a superior race walked the earth before ordinary men recurs in many cultures. These "super beings" possess extraordinary powers and journey down to Earth from the stars. Much speculation as to whether belief systems have originated from these "super beings" has been rife. It may be that the hero who embarks upon the quest is seeking to renew an acquaintance with these god-like figures.

Aliens always have knowledge more advanced than we do. How else would they be able to travel vast distances across space to Earth? Extra-terrestrial visitors who possess some object of supernatural powers would seem more than likely. To the hero, this would be seen as a great treasure and the physical representation of his search. As another path towards our understanding of the Grail and its origins, this is as likely as any.

My own Quest began in those far-off times. The spark of a lifelong involvement in the "magickal world" was kindled for me then. I deliberately do not use the word "spiritual" in this context. A term such as "spiritual path" has been used too often in the lexicon of the New Age. The phrase has become so devalued that along Glastonbury High Street in the twenty-first century, it is as devoid of meaning as "love and peace."

IX. DARK TIMES

"THE WOUNDED MAN HAS A BETTER VIEW OF
THE BATTLE THAN THOSE STILL SHOOTING."

— WALKER PERCY

Reputable manuals of occult instruction warn the initiate never to perform magick except in the name of the highest powers. This, in the Qabalah, is the Sephira of Kether. If the aspiring practitioner is tempted to work with elemental powers, he runs the risk of attracting demonic forces from the lower astral planes. The medieval magician with his grimoires to evoke devils is now almost a cliché, yet some errant souls are still tempted to dabble when they should leave well alone. It is from these murky realms that spells and curses take their power. The *raison d'être* of the Holy Grail is about as far from these things as it is possible to be.

Mention is made of *Chastel Merveille* in the Arthurian tales. This may be the residence built by Ygerna, the mother of Arthur, at the death of Uther Pendragon. Another tradition asserts that it is the residence of Klingsor, an evil magician and that Chastel Merveille represents a perverted version of the Grail Castle. The place has an apparent correspondence with the planet Pluto, the most mysterious and arcane planet in the astrological heavens. In its higher vibration, it represents a resolute search for spiritual perfection, while its lower energies can manifest in violence and tyranny. It has been posited by astrologers that, since the early 1930s, the vibrations of Pluto have influenced the collective unconscious of nations. This era certainly saw the rise of Hitler and other equally odious despots.

The Black Sun

Historians may attribute the rise of Hitler in 1930s Germany solely to social or economic causes. To account for the god-like status given to the self-styled Führer requires a different thesis. It is certain that the meteoric rise of the Nazi party was deftly engineered by the use of propaganda. One of the most chilling efforts in this campaign was *The Triumph of the Will*, a documentary film of the Nuremberg rally of 1935. Carefully orchestrated military displays were intercut with archetypal images that purportedly reflected the Third Reich. Edited by the director Leni Riefenstahl, the result was a compelling montage that portrayed Hitler and the Nazis as a messiah surrounded by his disciples.

Nordic myths could, with a minimum of manipulation, be adapted to the image of the Aryan super-race. Beowulf is the most obvious example, and the exploits of heroes and great warriors are not far behind. To die for the cause is a noble outcome, particularly if the souls of the dead are transported to Valhalla by the Valkyrie. It is a world of Fire and Ice that has little room for compromise. Within this testosterone-fuelled fantasy, "might is right."

Wagner used many Nordic myths and legends in his operas. *The Ring of Nibelung* features Wotan, the King of the Gods along with other deities in the pantheon. Hitler was a great admirer of Wagner. Although in his works, the composer's themes are undeniably centered around love and passion, the Führer probably saw the operas as an embodiment of his future vision for Germany. The sympathy between Hitler and Wagner, supposedly based on shared racist views, is still a controversial issue. Wagner's operas were not permitted to be staged in Israel until 2001, indicating the intensity of the reaction to his works after World War II.

The opinion that the Nazis used occult powers to gain their political ends is a view that has been posited for several decades. Is this simply a convenient excuse for the perpetrating of inhuman and savage acts and a denial of any personal responsibility? Such an insidious doctrine, to attribute supernatural means to the *modus operandi* of the Nazi monster, implies that all manner of horrific events can somehow be trivialized or explained away.

Inevitably, the term "black magick" features in these accusations. In any circumstance, this is a misnomer. Magick is never "black" nor "white"—it is a neutral force. The motives of the magician may be interpreted as being "good" or "evil," but magick has no moral stance *per se*. The shibboleth of duality is being raised once more and obscures the light of reason.

To employ highly emotive words such as "Satanism" or "Lucifer" in connection with Heinrich Himmler—the head of the SS—is the province of sensationalist websites. It cannot be denied that he was, with Reinhardt Heydrich, instrumental in implementing the "Final Solution"—that was his role in the Nazi hierarchy. A taste for genocide was not what drove Himmler; his overriding obsession was in acquiring and sustaining his own worldly power.

The Nazi High Command was riven with intrigue and betrayal. Himmler was determined, having gained such enviable heights, not to fall from grace. To Hitler, he appeared as one who was in accord with his vision of the "master race" no matter that Himmler's methods of achieving that end were extraordinarily diverse.

In 1935, Himmler inaugurated an organization named *Der Ahnenerbe*. Herman Wirth, an anthropologist, was its first president. The covert purpose of this organization was to establish that the Aryan races were superior to any other. Himmler travelled to Finland to meet a group of sorcerers in the belief they would inform him that the Nordic races once ruled the known world. Subsequent expeditions to Sweden, the Middle East, and to France (to view cave paintings) were all devised to confirm Himmler's thesis.

The cost of several of these junkets was sponsored by German banks. Other trips to Bolivia, the Canary Islands, and Crimea were planned but never came to fruition. In 1939, a celebrated journey to Tibet was undertaken. Its purpose was to gather statistics concerning the physique of the Tibetan people in an effort to prove their Nordic origins.

Guido Karl Anton List was an Austrian occultist born in the nineteenth century. He was a follower of Madame Blavatsky and a scholar and poet of some distinction. His visions of Wotan as a child and his discovery that the worship of this Sun god had been widespread among the Saxons spurred his later research into Nordic spirituality.

In the eighth and ninth centuries, the emperor Charlemagne had ruthlessly persecuted the Pagan tribes of Europe. His mission was to convert all Europe to Christianity. He was so successful that subsequently, the Catholic Church had no difficulty in obliterating all traces of Germanic devotions to Wotan.

List died in 1919 and his legacy has been unfairly linked to the pro-Aryan extremist groups that emerged in Germany during the 1930s. Among these were Liebenfel's cult of *Ariosophy* and the *Thule Society*. Of relevance to our study, if only in name, was the *Germanenorden Walvater of the Holy Grail*, founded by two enthusiasts—Sebotendorf and Brockhusen. Neither Hitler nor Himmler was a member of any of these groups.

The figure strongly associated with the occult who emerged in 1930s Germany was Karl Maria Wiligut. This plagiarist and charlatan had an extraordinarily powerful influence on the Nazi movement. An ex-member of the *Schlaraffia*—a quasi-Masonic lodge—Wiligut, by being appointed a knight and chancellor, had earned a certain reputation among German esoteric cults. As a member of the *Ordo Novi Templi* in Vienna, Wiligut claimed that the Bible had originally been written in German. Wiligut then attempted to establish his own *Irminic* religion at the expense of Wotanism, declaring that Irminism was the true religion of the German people.

In 1933, Himmler had been introduced to Wiligut. He was almost immediately inducted into the SS. His superior must have been impressed with Wiligut, as by 1936, he had attained the rank of *Brigadeführer* and was serving on Himmler's personal staff. He was appointed "Head of Archives" and was given significant responsibilities.

Herman Wirth was not impressed with Himmler's protégé. In a letter to Rudolf J. Mind, he described Wiligut as "a senile alcoholic." Diagnosed as a schizophrenic in 1939, Wiligut spent the war years in seclusion, dying in 1946. He did, however, leave a certain insidious legacy.

Wiligut devised his own set of "runes," adapting the genuine *futhark* (dating from 150 AD) that had been researched by Guido List. Himmler chose to adopt Wiligut's version for some of the Nazi insignia. The most recognizable, and infamous, are the *Sig* runes that were worn by the Schutzstaffel (SS).

Wiligut's other contribution was to provide Himmler with a state religion. The new creed was named *Volkisch* which fitted neatly into Hitler's *Volkstümlich* ("populist") plan for German culture and society. This creed was intended to replace Christianity in Europe. Hitler gave his approval to this scheme even before it was finalized. Based upon Germany's supposed Germanic Pagan heritage, many of Wiligut's ideas were incorporated in it.

Establishing an actual "Centre of the New World" was paramount in this ideology, an ambition which was to be partially realised by Himmler. Wewelsburg Castle in Westphalia, north of the Rhine, was chosen as the location. Its attraction was that several archaeological investigations into early Germanic history were being carried out in the area.

Himmler set about inaugurating a "movement" whose symbol was to be a twelve-spoked Sun wheel. This has come to be known as the "Black Sun" partly because of its sinister overtones. It has been said that the sign of the swastika was derived from it, but that symbol is much older, occurring in India and Ancient Egypt.

A mosaic of the Black Sun was set into the ground floor room in the north tower of the castle. Green with a gold disc in the centre, the design was set against a grey background. Known as the *Obergruppenführer Hall*, it was here that Himmler and his generals met to converse and meditate upon the future of the Third Reich. Their number was thirteen, Himmler being the thirteenth member of the group. This arrangement was deliberately created as an echo of the Round Table.

By 1943, it was evident that the war was not going well for Hitler and many projects within Germany were abandoned. Thus, the grandiose plans for Wewelsburg, which included a massive reconstruction of the North Tower and several parts of the rest of the castle, never came to fruition.

The Sacred Lance

Supposedly, the "Spear of Longinus" is the weapon that pierced Christ's side at the crucifixion. Along with the Crown of Thorns, this has been regarded as one of the holiest of relics, next only to the Grail itself. The Lance in the Grail legend is one of the Hallows and appears in the Grail Procession at Carbonek. It is the same lance that wounds the Fisher King.

From the seventh century onwards, when a pilgrim reported as to having seen it, the Lance has a habit of appearing and reappearing. The tip was supposedly broken off in the sixth or seventh century and this became a separate object of veneration. Thus, two versions of the treasure (as well as several others claiming to be the original) have emerged over the centuries. The Lance that is held in the Vatican was once considered to be the only genuine version. Another, "Constantine's Lance" as it is known, is regarded as the most authentic. This was part of the imperial regalia at the coronation of the Holy Roman emperors.

A youthful Adolf Hitler was one of the many who gazed upon Constantine's Lance in the *Welichtes Schatzkammer* Museum in Vienna. Its heritage, that of being held by forty-five successive emperors even before Charlemagne possessed it, was impressive. The sight of the Spear certainly had an impact upon the future dictator. Hitler was further inspired when he learned that Frederick the Great (1194-1250), who founded the Order of the Teutonic Knights, once owned the Lance. Did he know then that it would one day be in his possession?

By 1935, the Nazi Party had established an overwhelming political power in Germany. Hitler then began his bid for world power by extending the existing borders of Germany, and the annexation of Austria in 1938 was his first coup. As soon as he and his armies entered Vienna, Hitler had the Hapsburg Crown Jewels transferred to Nuremberg. He now owned the Lance! He renamed his treasure "The Spear of Destiny" as he was convinced this was the omen that his hour had come. The following year, he ordered the invasion of Poland, an act of aggression which brought about World War II. The tale has a fitting conclusion. U.S. soldiers discovered the Lance on April 30th, 1945. A matter of hours later, Hitler committed suicide in his Berlin bunker.

Reluctant Nazi

The life of Otto Rahn makes for an extraordinary tale. A very minor figure in the history of the first half of the twentieth century, Rahn epitomizes the conflict between idealism and political power. Many were victims of the Nazi ideological machine, including some figures of greater significance than Rahn, yet his story makes for a poignant tragedy. The path of enchantment led to his inevitable demise—a very Arthurian theme, and the brief saga of his life still exerts a melancholy fascination.

Otto Rhan was born in Michelstadt, the town of St. Michael. Its pre-Christian title was Siegfried. The area is the Odenwalt, the forests of Odin. Rahn was raised alongside two strong traditions, and he would come to identify strongly with both Parsifal and Wotan.

The moment his mother introduced him to the Grail romances, he set out upon his own Quest. After he had gained a degree in Philology and History, he was determined to be a writer and researcher of the Grail. To allay his immediate expenses, he secured a small income as a teacher in Geneva. He later became a follower of Madame Blavatsky, though whether he was ever a member of the Theosophical Society is uncertain.

Rahn was convinced that the Holy Vessel was located in France and that its whereabouts were somehow linked to the Cathars.

Rahn's theories concerning its heritage went further than any previous speculations. He was convinced that the Druids were the forerunners of the Cathar Parfaits. The doctrines of Gnosticism and Manichaeism were, he believed, the basis of the Cathar tradition. He also believed that their secret wisdom had been preserved in the songs of the Troubadours.

All this might simply have been the stuff of some obscure tome, written down and then forgotten, fated to forever languish in some desk drawer. But Rahn was no mere cerebral investigator, and in 1931, he set out for the Pyrenees. There, in the caves beneath the fortress of Montsegur, Rahn probed and excavated among the rocks. He was convinced that the "Cathar Church" was the "Church of the Grail," one that had associations with the *Fideles d'Amour* revered by the Troubadours.

His investigations were aided by Antonin Gadal, a local mystic, historian, and local landowner. Upon his property were over sixty caves and perhaps the pair were equally fired by the dream that they might discover the cup. Gadal's goal, however, seems to have been more in the nature of an inner search. His research was as diligent as Rahn's but he published nothing in his lifetime. Gadal was known for his often-expressed belief that a link existed between the Grail, the Cathars, and Rosicrucianism. After Rahn's death, there were accusations that he had plagiarized Gadal's research.

Two years after the Pyrenean expedition, Rahn published his findings in *Kreuzzug gegen den Gral*— "Crusade against the Grail." A crucial passage in the book revived the debate as to whether the Grail's actual physical form was a stone. Why did the ancients regard certain natural objects as sacred? Stone is the one material that from the first has been employed in creating "meaningful" and what were presumed to be "permanent" constructions. Endless examples of megalithic monuments still exist in the world. Crystals and meteorites too have been revered over the centuries—the *Kaaba* at Mecca is one example of this practice. We may suggest that Ayers Rock, on a grander scale, is another.

Rahn's conception of the Grail combined several traditions. He actually believed it was made of emerald—either one perfect stone with one hundred and forty-four facets or the same number of small emerald tablets. Each was engraved, he believed, with inscriptions that resembled runes. Rahn was anxious to combine his deeply felt attachments to several traditions within the Grail. To this end, there are elements of the Nordic, Arthurian, and Celtic in his vision.

His abiding attachment to the Cathars is the strongest theme in *Crusade*. His affection for the chivalric code, as it is celebrated in the songs of the troubadours, entranced him. These troupes of minstrels and storytellers came originally from Occitania, the idyllic French kingdom of the twelfth century. Their tradition of storytelling and music may well date from an earlier era as Joseph Campbell explains.

> *"During the tenth century, a brilliant period of romance production... converted the inheritance into an important contemporary force. Celtic bards went out to the courts of Christian Europe; Celtic themes were rehearsed by the Pagan Scandinavian scalds. A great part of our European fairy lore, as well as the foundation of the Arthurian tradition, traces back to this first great creative period of Occidental romance."[59]*

The most significant episode in Cathar history is obviously the demise of their order. Rahn gives a detailed account of the fall of Montsegur based on the songs of the troubadours and local folk traditions. The following passage needs to be quoted in its entirety:

> *"When the walls of Montsegur were still standing, the Cathars, the Pure Ones, kept the Holy Grail inside them. Montsegur was in danger; the armies of Lucifer were before its walls. They wanted to take the Grail to insert it again into the diadem of their Prince, from where it had broken off and fallen to Earth during the fall of the angels. At this most crucial point, a white dove came from the sky and split the Tabor (the local peak) in two. Esclarmonde, the keeper of the Grail, threw the precious relic into the mountain, where it was hidden. So they saved the Grail."[60]*

The text is rich in elements of Grail lore. "Esclarmonde," which means "Light of Crystal" or "Light of the World" in the Occitan language, was Esclarmonde de Foix, a fervent follower of the Cathar faith after she had been widowed in 1200. She was one of the minds behind the rebuilding of Montsegur Castle so that it would become the stronghold of the Cathars. Her charitable works were numerous and were a practical expression of her piety. She was also possessed of a formidable intellect, one strong enough to debate the Cathar cause with the Catholic Church. This was the last occasion before the Abigensian Crusade that the two factions met in some harmony.

The reference to the dove is of interest as it as an ancient symbol of transition from one state of consciousness to another. It is the spirit of heaven descending to Earth—a sacred message from above. The dove is essentially feminine and associated with Athena and Aphrodite. The Christian Grail is depicted with the dove of peace above the rim of the cup.

The darker reference to "the armies of Lucifer" would prove to be a terrible premonition of what was to follow in Rahn's beloved Germany. Already, the forces that would threaten to overrun Europe and the rest of the civilized world were gathering.

The success that Rahn expected would greet the publication of *Crusade* did not materialize. To his disappointment the work sold only five thousand copies throughout Germany. The income from this was not enough to allay his financial difficulties. This period in his life was one of terrible poverty and privation. He eked out an existence in Paris, continued to write, and persisted in negotiating to publish a French edition of *Crusade*.

The Caged Dove

In 1935, Rahn's fortunes appeared to dramatically change. He received a letter which offered what appeared to be a glorious sinecure. A promise of accommodation in Berlin, premises to work, the services of a secretary, and a subsidy of a thousand *Reichmarks* a month was offered. In return, he had simply to continue his Grail research. It all seemed too good to be true.

Full of curiosity, Rahn duly appeared at the door of 7, Prinz-Albrecht-Strasse in Berlin. He was more than astonished to be ushered into the presence of Heinrich Himmler. So, this was his anonymous benefactor! The head of the SS informed Rahn that he was most impressed with his book and invited him to write another. This would be *Luzifers Hofgesind*— "Lucifer's Court"—published in

1937. Rahn accepted the offer and arrangements were made for his future. His financial affairs in Paris were quietly settled for him and Otto Rahn moved to Berlin to join Himmler's personal staff.

Why was Himmler so convinced that Rahn could be of service to him and aid his future plans? It may have been that a passage in *Crusade against the Grail* was in complete accord with Himmler's most strongly held beliefs—the implication that the aristocracy of Languedoc (the area of Rahn's research) were of Nordic stock.

Rahn had also made an extensive exploration of the caverns—some massive—in the Sabarthez area. The walls of these were covered with Templar symbols as well as Cathar emblems. Rahn believed that the Templars, after they were disbanded, found refuge in the caves of the Pyrenees. Among his findings was a carving of the Sacred Lance. Knowing Hitler's obsession with this artifact, Himmler made sure that the Fuhrer was quickly informed. A gratified Hitler ensured that funds were available to enable Rahn's research to continue.

Did Himmler seriously believe that Rahn could lead him to the Grail? Did the head of the SS believe that if he possessed the actual cup, he could employ its power for his own ends? It seems likely. The Nazis had perverted science and technology in order to satisfy their lust for world domination. Why should they not employ a transcendental source of power as well if they could acquire it?

In 1936, Rahn travelled to Iceland, the cradle of Nordic myth, with a party of twenty under his leadership. When he returned to present his findings to Himmler, the latter more than praised his efforts. But he also issued an edict—Rahn must become a full member of the SS. Reluctantly, Otto agreed to do so. His reported rejoinder to his friends who saw him in Nazi uniform was, *"a man has to eat. What was I supposed to do, turn Himmler down?"*

In 1937, the work commissioned by Himmler appeared. *Luzifers Hofgesind*—Lucifer's Court. It contains direct references to the "Land of the Midnight Sun"—the Black Sun. Rahn quotes Jakob Bohme, the mystical writer of the seventeenth century, *"towards midnight, because the light is clear in the darkness..."* But this reads simply as a sop to Nazi ideology, Rahn's true concern is with a god of light. His "Lucifer" is the Celtic *Bel*, also personified as the Greek *Apollo*. His vision for Europe was not *volkisch*—chthonic, even parochial—it was something much more eternal. He wrote:

> *"What is that strength from above that conquers the power of death and hatred? Who can awaken a very lonely mankind after the twilight...so that we can rebuild society in selfless service, taking care not to destroy freedom, but to heal it?"*[61]

Rahn is identifying with the sacrificial god. Within two years, the role that he had made for himself would become a tragic reality.

Himmler was immensely pleased with Rahn's work. When published, five thousand copies of the book specially bound in leather were distributed to members of the SS. Rahn immediately began another project. This time, the subject was to be Prometheus. This work, Himmler insisted, was to be finished by the end of 1939. He was also working on a novel and a biography of Conrad of Marburg, the notorious inquisitor and persecutor of the Cathars. Rahn had asked permission from Himmler to leave Berlin and work at his cottage in the Black Forest. However, it eventually made little difference where he was, forces were swiftly gathering to bring about his end.

Openly homosexual and possibly with a Jewish ancestry, Rahn's position had always been precarious. Inevitably, he was denounced by his superiors in the SS. In 1939, a sham "marriage" was orchestrated to convince the Nazi hierarchy that he had been sexually reformed. Karl Wiligut and Himmler were even guests at the wedding.

But it was not enough to satisfy those who held the real power over him, and Rahn was given an unenviable choice. He would either be assassinated by an SS "hit-squad," or he could take his own life. Rahn chose the latter and set off on his last pilgrimage. Almost to the day of the fall of Montsegur, his frozen body was found on the Wilder Kaiser mountain in Austria. He was thirty-five years old. In his heart and mind, Rahn had returned to his true love—the Grail of the Cathars. A contemporary description of his body when it was recovered recalls that his features appeared:

"...sacred, (and have) the saintliness of a hermit, of a sage. The face displayed a great gentleness and softness; there was no sign of agony."[62]

Rahn would never experience the years that followed. Many believed that the apocalypse had finally come. In many cultures, the poetic visions of the end of the world are often the most evocative of ancient writings. Revelation speaks of the Armageddon in chilling verse, while the Norse canon describes Ragnarök, a time when,

"...the watchman of the gods shall blow the shrieking horn, the warrior sons of Othin will be summoned to the final battle. From all quarters the gods, giants, demons, dwarfs, and elves will be riding for the field. The World Ash, Yggdrasil, will tremble, and nothing will then be without fear in heaven and earth."[63]

The imagery of the *Poetic Edda* is even more stark in its sentiments.

"The sun turns black, earth sinks into the sea,
The hot stars down from heaven are whirled;
Fierce grows the steam and the life-feeding flame,
Till fire leaps high about heaven itself."[64]

The opening line seems terribly prophetic, yet from all this emerges a new world. Perhaps our own apocalypse was in the twentieth century when the Four Horsemen rode roughshod over all that had been held dear. We still live in testing times. Let us hope that an even better world will soon emerge. As always, Joseph Campbell offers a wise commentary:

"Apocalypse does not point to a fiery Armageddon but to the fact that our ignorance and our complacency are coming to an end."[65]

X. AQUARIAN AGE

"IT'S HOW YOUR SOUL IS DOING IN ITS PATH
TO ETERNITY, NOT HOW YOUR BODY IS DOING
ON ITS PATH THROUGH THIS LIFE, THAT'S
IMPORTANT."

— KEN KESEY

According to Avicenna, an eleventh-century philosopher, the universe consists of a chain of beings each promoting life to the one below. If the chain is not infinite, and Avicenna believed it was not, then it must terminate in a being who bestows life upon the rest. This existence, not being contingent to any other entity in the universe, is seen as the primal cause and responsible for the creation of the universe. Avicenna had thus proposed the first ontological and cosmological argument for the existence of God.

It may be that we could substitute the "Grail" for "God." The holy vessel has always been with us in one form or another. We have seen that in its history it has assumed many guises, been vilified and worshipped, and even abandoned and repressed. The Grail assumes many guises and still it returns as it always will. It is a symbol of eternity and as such cannot be commanded. The biblical sentiment *"it bloweth where it listeth"* is often quoted with regard to the nature of the Grail.[66] The Grail has its own agenda. It remains hidden, away from the hustle and bustle of the world, as Arthur remains sleeping. This is not yet the moment for the return of either.

Being Informed

As we have learned, the first hint of the Grail came in an era when all knowledge was contained within an oral tradition. With the advent of writing came a new consciousness brought about by the new way in which ideas could be conveyed. What must be considered is that manuscripts were rare items. Books, which were basically collections of manuscripts, even more so. Only a minority of the population was literate, thus increasing the exclusivity of the information contained in the written word.

In those far off days, words owned power, much more than they do now. Words were the dominion of the powerful—lawmakers, historians, and magicians. The sentiments that they uttered resonated with the energy of the message that was being transmitted. To speak was to be heard and to be listened to. In a few millennia, the nature of the medium has changed irrevocably. Now it is form and not content that determines what is disseminated into the aether. Sean O'Brien has an interesting insight into the way this approach has changed the way an author writes:

> *"...the cinematic imagination has for some time been feeding back into work written for the page, often with the effect of lending a novel the preliminary character of a film waiting to happen, so that the text becomes a series of cues on which to base a visible world, rather than a creation existing in its own right."*[67]

We live in an age when access to information has never been greater, yet freedom of thought seems to have diminished at the same rate. The 1960s marked the dawn of the electronic age when Marshal McLuhan memorably informed us that, *"The Medium is the Message"* (the pun in the title being apposite, but apparently accidental). His thesis was that form was more important than content, in a way that had never been known before. He was right, and the unfortunate result has been that in the arts, style, pastiche, and the insidious doctrine of post-modernism have replaced real creativity. Commercial interests in league with a sophisticated political materialism have conspired to destroy genuine debate.

More alarmingly, in our schools and universities, passive instruction does lip-service for teaching. Although seen as necessary to "success," "education" has abandoned the pursuit of knowledge, an exercise that should lead to understanding. The filmmaker and one time Monty Python animator Terry Gilliam has this to say:

> *"I really want to encourage...a kind of magic. I love the term magic realism...because it says certain things. It's about expanding how you see the world. I think we live in an age where we're just hammered, hammered, to think this is what the world is. Television's saying, everything's saying 'That's the world.' And it's not the world. The world is a million possible things."*[68]

Our other failing is the speed at which the majority embraces a clichéd view of the world and is content to do so. The corporate mind is stuffed with the mundane and the predictable. Our desire to impose a quantitative schema denies the mysterious essence that is at the heart of our world. We are no longer curious or surprised by the world. Technology blurs the difference between reality and an "image of reality." Thus, deception and manipulation may so easily be employed to control the common mind.

It is a sinister situation, one that we need to be aware of, and one that should be constantly fought. We are dominated by the very technology that we once naively supposed would be our servant—the microchip rules society. An unstoppable progress has seen to it that computers, mobile phones, and all the rest will now never go away. We live in an era that has the mind as its matrix. Our neurons work at full stretch, and we have built a new world, but we have lost the imagination to build our own temple. The digital experience offers unlimited choice, but only as a substitute for invention.

The New Age

Previous generations of occultists would have been bemused by the New Age. The pioneers of the magickal tradition naturally espoused Arthur and the Quest, and we should be grateful to them for depicting the Grail as an inspiration. These men and women of magick, often as heroic as the figures they espoused, knew how significant the Arthurian tales were to the spirituality of the West. Often larger-than-life, like Dion Fortune or Aleister Crowley, or retiring and hermit-like as Colonel Seymour, Christine Hartley and Bill Gray led the vanguard.

It is certainly evident why a "New Age" philosophy has developed. Changing ideas of our spiritual and physical relationship with the universe have resulted in questioning our role on Earth. Do we see ourselves as pioneers on the frontiers of technology and ideology or as champions of ecology and humanity? If so, our courage and spiritual principles may reflect, in microcosm, those of King Arthur and The Quest for the Holy Grail.

Isis Unveiled

Isis never fights, but she is always a victorious queen. Her secrets lie within the Grail, and they cannot be taken from her. Never is the Grail abstract in the sense of a mathematical formula or an abstract painting, the latter being subject to any number of random interpretations. When a sacred image is truly perceived, he who beholds it becomes that image entirely.

The revelation of the Grail to any mortal is accompanied by a mixture of emotions, some impossible to communicate. The term is "ineffability," but such an experience cannot be expressed satisfactorily in words. As William James describes:

> "...it is the experience of something hitherto unknown. It is something inconceivable. So the mind cannot find words to describe such an overwhelming experience. In a sense it defines communication, which in its turn can lead to feelings of

disappointment and failure, because more than anything in the world one wants to share this feeling."[69]

James goes on to detail the results of the experience—the most profound is the joy that accompanies liberty. Such an enormous relief gives rise to a psychological transformation that is amazing. Apart from the visible signs of ecstasy in laughter, dancing, or tears of bliss, the psyche is permanently altered. Inner Reality has radically altered because it has been dramatically restored to harmony. A solemnity is experienced; there is trust in the rightness of things and awe in the face of creation. Greatest of all is the realisation that fear and distress are forever in the past. When a religious experience is collated and organized it loses its power—it becomes orthodoxy.

Eternal Presence

Throughout our study, we have examined and evaluated all manner of explanations for the way in which the universe behaves. Towards the end of his life, the renowned author John Michell was moved to write:

"God is always one and the same, whereas science is an endless diversity, a cacophony of theories and opinions...quite incapable of deciding on the nature of things..."[70]

Our existence is a puzzle, yet we have a duty as sentient and sapient beings to investigate and evaluate all that we perceive. Because we possess both reason *and* intuition, we are at a tremendous mental advantage. Perhaps we have access to all knowledge—everything that has ever been known or will be known. The mathematician and astronomer Pierre-Simon Laplace, writing in 1814, suggested that:

"An intellect which at a certain moment would know all forces that set nature in motion, and all positions of all items of which nature is composed, if this intellect were also vast enough to submit these data to analysis, it would embrace in a single formula the movements of

the greatest bodies of the universe and those of the tiniest atom; for such an intellect nothing would be uncertain and the future just like the past would be present before its eyes. "[71]

The Grail, above all other symbols, epitomizes the joining together of all the elements in the universe and the concord that accompanies it. As Jung remarked, *"The psyche and matter are two different aspects of the same thing."* The Grail is a great gift to us *in the world*. We must venture forth and discover this template of the world.

Schopenhauer could have been describing the Grail when in 1819 he wrote:

"Although as a rule the absurd culminates, and it seems impossible for the voice of the individual ever to penetrate through the chorus of foolers and fooled, still there is left to the genuine works of all times a quite peculiar, silent, slow, and powerful influence; and as if by a miracle, we see them rise at last out of the turmoil like a balloon that floats up out of the thick atmosphere of this globe into purer regions. Having once arrived there, it remains at rest, and no one can any longer draw it down again. "[72]

The Grail is a symbol of all that we desire to cherish and preserve during our sojourn on this planet—our home. The universe responds to strength, never to weakness, and the resolve that is shown by those engaged upon the Quest is rewarded with "the peace that passes understanding." The Grail heals our pain no matter how grievous it may be.

Beyond the state of ecstasy that the Grail brings lies the ineffable. It is a sight that we should not experience in all its totality, for it may be too much for us. The Grail exists in an infinite number of forms and perhaps we are shown the one that is best suited to ourselves—a "likeness" of the Holy Vessel that best reflects our progress along our path. The Grail, with its knowledge of the soul of every one of us, is a symbol of the unseen world. It is also a go-between—at the same time communicating with us and the world; it is, in Jungian terms, the anima communicating with the ego. The "me" that we fondly believe is ourselves, is better off in the role of a scanning device—a reporter.

Great Love

Can the power of the Sun God and the Moon Maiden bring equilibrium and joy to the world once more? And are we warriors still, or sorcerers or kings? Is there still a priestess or a queen among us?

> *"...there is a climate of expectation in the world—expectation sustained, contemplated and intensified through the course of the centuries. Without being nourished and directed from above, the energy of human expectation alone would have exhausted itself long ago. But it is not exhausted; rather, on the contrary, it is growing. This is because it aspires to a reality and not an illusion."[73]*

In May 2010, Uranus moved on from the passive sign of Pisces to begin a new cycle in Aries, the first sign of the zodiac. Aries is the Ram—cardinal Fire, the pioneer, the hero, and the leader. If there was ever a time for the will to blend with the spark of inspiration, it is now.

The Grail is an ocean of silence, communicating through the heart. If we love others unconditionally, we reflect the greatest virtue of the Grail. If the Grail can be summed up in one word, it is "love." St. Paul remarked that the foolishness of God is wiser than the wisdom of men—the Divine Will always triumphs.

We have come full circle since the time of Arthur and we are now poised at the beginning of our own Quest. It is a journey to Avalon every bit as purposeful as that embarked upon by the questing knights. Wood, lake, and cavern all contain mystery in the land we pass through. After the Hallows have been returned in the Faery Autumn, peace will again rule in this blessed kingdom.

We must not stray from that path until we see Arthur return to us in all his glory. All we can hope for is that each one of us becomes a "Holder of the Holy Grail." In knowing Arthur, we experience the "nobility of divinity." We walk in the footsteps of those who went before, sometimes alone, often wronged, but always in the company of the gods.

APPENDIX

KING ARTHUR, THE HOLY GRAIL, & THE MYSTICAL KING

"A hero is a person we don't know much about. He or she seems to embody an era, usually one from the past, and, as Fenelon said the past is a strange thing, the further away from it you stand, the bigger it looks."

—Eric Griffiths, Review of *Troilus and Cressida*

"'A warrior cannot be helpless,' he said, 'Or bewildered or frightened, not under any circumstances. For a warrior there is time only for his impeccability; everything else drains his power, impeccability replenishes it.'"

—Carlos Castenada, *Tales of Power*

"One of the lessons of open minded research is that there is a wrongness which leads to rightness more effectively than rightness itself."

—Geoffrey Ashe, *The Quest for Arthur's Britain*

Arthur of the Britons[74]

William of Malmesbury, writing *Deeds of the Kings of England* in 1125, described Arthur *"as one who has sustained his tottering country and gave the shattered minds of his fellow citizens an edge for war."* The years before the Saxon invasion were looked upon as a time *"...with abundance beyond the memory of an earlier age..."*[75] but from 430 AD onward, invaders from Denmark and the Zuyder Zee descended on this land, which by the middle of the ninth century was effectively conquered, leaving only small and scattered enclaves of Romano-British inhabitants. Thus, we would conclude that all marked resistance died with Arthur. Geoffrey Ashe makes the point that over six hundred years, the character of the invader had changed. *"The Anglo-Saxons who finally won were no longer the murderous pirates of the fifth century."*[76] But invaders they were, and the character of these islands changed completely with their coming.

The *Annales Cambriae* describes *Artorius* or Arthur as a princely aristocrat, one who replaced Ambrosius as the supreme commander of the British. Arthur's title of *dux bellorum* went undisputed as did more exotic titles, "emperor, the ruler in the toil of battle."

Born in the latter half of the fifth-century AD, Arthur was a leader of such renown that his followers, *"bold men of Arthur's who hewed with steel,"* would have gladly died for him. He had also a reputation for keeping a hospitable house. In the story of *Culhwch and Owen*, it seems all manner of delights were on offer at his hall.

> *"...hot peppered chops...and wine brimming over, and delectable songs...a woman to sleep with thee..."*

Among Arthur and his men, battle appears to have been the *raison d'être* of their existence. Fighting men inevitably did not live long and *"in battle they made women widows,"* so life was stark and death never far away.[77]

In his first encounter with the Saxons at Badon Hill (or Mount Badon), Arthur defeated them. A reference to Arthur and the enemy, *"none slew them but he alone"* in *History of Britain* by Nennius, is an early indication of his reputation. The same account also more than hints that Arthur had divine aid (in this case, Christian), an oft mentioned occurrence. Arthur, it appears, does not have an untarnished reputation, and as Ashe explains "*...the Welsh monastic tradition would seem to have been unfriendly toward Arthur...*" seeing him as "*a hard-bargaining warrior chief out for what he can get.*"[78] Arthur begins more to resemble our idea of a hard-bitten fighter, and as Ashe goes on to explain:

> "*Some such person existed...to deny his reality would solve no problems...Arthur was not king of Britain...we may picture him as a rustic noble, born in the 470s...by an unusual flair for leadership he attracted a following...but despite victory, his standing was never secure.*"[79]

This description of an inspired but flawed soldier, concerned only with battle and not the niceties of diplomacy, fits in with an idea of Arthur being exactly the right man in the right place. One who inspires his men and leads by example, a man who never appears to be cowed by the enemy and who shows his people that the invader can be vanquished. It is no wonder Arthur has gained a place in the history of this island. Naturally, we revere those who defend us against the enemy, and with Boadicea, Arthur was our first military hero.[80] Four hundred years later, Alfred the Great was to defend us against the Danes.

Once *in situ*, the invading Saxons came to refer to the Britons as *wealh* or *wylisc*, in modern English—*Wales*. The later claim for an exclusively Welsh Arthur probably springs from a desire in the Middle Ages by the oppressed people of Wales to have a hero of their own. *The Mabinogion* (based on *Tales from the White Book of Rhydderch)*, a thirteenth-century manuscript, although known to be substantially corrupted, is the only surviving record of Celtic history. Arthur is mentioned in five of its tales. Depicted as a king rather than a warrior prince (Morris describes him as "*the first medieval king*"), Arthur is married to Gwenhwvar (Guinevere) who bears him two sons.[81] Much is made of being constantly at his camp at Caer Llion (*Caerleon*—The Lion's Place).

Geoffrey Ashe lists one hundred and four references to places associated with Arthur, from the Northeast of Scotland to the very tip of Cornwall. As well as the Welsh claim to him, there is also a Northern school, for in Scotland, Arthur is the Hunter or *Ardu*, the dark one.

In his account of the period, Morris rightly questions the long-established view of the Dark Ages as a period when *"men were ignorant, illiterate and brutish, authors of a dismal regression from the elegant splendours of Rome"* and comments on this school, that *"darkness lies in the eye of the beholder."*[82] Though it is still not easy to pull out many plums of fact from beneath a historical crust, still surprisingly opaque.

Fired by evidence that Arthur was a West Country warrior, *"Always I had been sure that Avalon and Camelot looked forwards as well as backwards. They were keys."*[83] In the 1960s, Geoffrey Ashe organised the *Camelot Project*, a serious archaeological scheme to determine if South Cadbury in Somerset was the site of the famed "castle." Cadbury has always owned the principle claim to the title, the local names naming:

> *"The summit plateau at the crest of the ridge (is) 'King Arthur's Palace.' One of the two widely separated wells in the hillside is 'King Arthur's Well'…a general notion that the hill is hollow… there is an iron gate, or maybe a golden one, and if you come at the right moment, it stands open and you can see King Arthur asleep inside."*[84]

Arthur's Hunting Path is a route from Cadbury to Glastonbury Tor. Legends insist that it is the route taken by Arthur and the Wild Hunt. Nicholas Mann has reckoned that:

> *"As this is the path aligned to the extreme rising and setting points of the moon it is probable the hunt rides along it every 18.61 years. In essence the observer can see from Cadbury the most northerly setting point of the moon over the Tor, and from the Tor the most southerly rising point of the moon over Cadbury."*[85]

Other associations that link the Tor with the Moon appear later in the work. To return to Cadbury and its environs, it is also possible that the battle of Camlann, Arthur's last stand, was fought nearby as a mass grave was found at this site. Ashe concluded that a chieftain of some reputation had his camp at South Cadbury who could have been Arthur, and there is no reason to suppose it was not him.

Included in Ashe's seminal work *The Quest for Arthur's Britain* was an article by C.A. Ralegh Rawford, in which he noted that *"... on Glastonbury Tor, the hill above the abbey, he (Radford) had indeed found a small settlement with pottery from the fifth or sixth century."*[86] If Arthur did occupy the Tor in the sixth century, it was likely that he would have established his camp on the east and south sides of the summit, so this find may go some way to confirming his being there. And as has been mentioned, Arthur may have been *persona non grata* with the monkish community and so might have chosen not to associate himself with the nearby Abbey. That more evidence has not been discovered of such an encampment may be due to all traces of it having been destroyed by a subsequent Anglo-Saxon settlement or habitations in the Middle Ages. Another possibility is that *Melwas* had his camp there. The tale of his kidnapping Guinevere and holding her on the Tor until she was rescued by her husband is part of Arthurian lore.

Ronald Hutton suggests another important historical role that the Tor may have played, as it:

> *"...is intervisible with two other prominent Somerset hills, Cadbury castle...and Brent Knoll. From Brent Knoll it is possible to see across the Severn estuary to the Welsh coast, and the hill of Dinas Powys...they might have functioned as a chain of lookout posts...between which alarm signals could pass...the identity of the enemy...is very clear: the Irish."*[87]

Again commending Morris, Ronald Hutton proposes that his fellow historian:

> *"provided a detailed narrative of the hero's career based on medieval documents from many periods...Morris called him (Arthur) the last Roman emperor of Britain and asserted that his rule had formed the identities of the English and Welsh nations."*[88]

Thus, a great warrior of a millennium and a half ago lived. None at that time, perhaps least of all Arthur, could have predicted the impact his relatively brief appearance on our soil would have upon the history and the soul of Great Britain.

The King is Dead, Long Live the King.

Arthur was to have an essential part in Celtic tradition. *"The Celts gift to the Western world was one of magic and imagination,"* as Grigsby has it.[89] The birth of Arthur, as it came to be related, was the stuff of legend, involving a *"Celtic equivalent of the Leda and the Swan tale."* The account of his death, as described by Geoffrey of Monmouth, is characteristically more sober.[90]

The Battle of Camlann was fought in either 537 or 539 at the end of a campaign against renewed invasion by the Anglo-Saxons. Of Camlann, Geoffrey of Monmouth records, *"...the renowned King Arthur himself was wounded deadly and was borne unto the island of Avalon..."* But where was Avalon? Both William of Malmesbury and Cardoc of Llancarfan knew the British name for Glastonbury—*Ynys Witrin*—yet neither suggests any association between Glastonbury and Avalon. The etymological puzzles that appear when the names are coupled seem endless. The Romans named Glastonbury *Avallonia* and the Anglo-Saxons called the place *Glaesting-byrig*, so already we are back where we started. The research of Louis H. Gray produced *Glassonby, Glasson,* and *Glastincodunom* as stages in a transformation to *Glaesting-byrig*. By comparison, the origins of *Avalon* seem relatively straightforward. The Cornish *aval* is apple, *avallen* is apple tree, and the Welsh is *aballon*. The Irish *ablach* means "rich in apples" and *Avallach* is "the place of apples."

> *"According to The Triads of Ireland, three things were regarded as especially holy 'an apple tree, a hazel bush, and a sacred grove.' An old Gaelic story tells of a youth in Paradise who ate of a golden apple which nevertheless remained a whole apple...an indication of the imperishability and the divinity of the apple...the apple was the fruit of longevity."*[91]

The enigma returns when we learn that Avalon (or *Annwvyn* or *Annwyn*) is a mystical otherworld called the Isle of Apples. "Apple howling" or *wassailing* is carried out on Twelfth Night to drive away the bad spirits of winter and encourage the vegetation gods. Dion Fortune insisted that *"literally and poetically"* it was *"the isle of the glassy wave...(and) Avallonia, was the mead of the apple...".*[92] The many references to the Isle of Glass, or the Crystal Isle were perhaps refined by Graves' suggestion that the place was the male equivalent of the White Goddess' domain. She is the New Moon, symbol of birth and growth who commands a sepulchre of quartz and cites the glass castles of Irish and Welsh legend as her island shrines. *"Their connexion with death and with the Moon-goddess (is) preserved in the popular superstition that it is unlucky to see the Moon through glass."*[93] Another reference is provided by Geoffrey of Monmouth, who speaks of:

> *"The Island of Apples, which men call the Fortunate Isle, is so named because it produces all things of itself. The field there have no need of framers to plough them, and Nature alone provides all cultivation... The earth of its own accord brings forth... all things in superabundance."*

The flat, undulating landscape of Somerset does not appeal to all, and coming upon high ground on a journey across the moors, be it a peak, tump, or tor (such as Brent Knoll or Burrow Mump) is a revelation. Settlements grow up in the shadow that gathers about these places. Of the soggy peat below, it seems incredible that the successful draining of Sedgemoor (one of the largest tracts of moorland in the county) was completed a mere seventy years ago. Until then, the winter floods would regularly appear at the foot of Glastonbury Tor. In Roman times, the tide profoundly affected the amount of water lying in Somerset and made it a land of *"crumbling shores, doubtful paths, fickle islands, and spectral marshes."*[94] This mysterious and often inhospitable land was to become the setting for one of the most potent and sustained legends in the history of Great Britain. As John Michell remarks, *"...in the Somerset countryside every episode in the adventures of King Arthur's knights in quest of the Grail has its physical location..."*[95] The West of England has too a significance, for as Bligh Bond observed:

> *"...the flow of spiritual forces is westward, following and impelling the forces of material things. By a law of revolution reinforced from all points in the spiritual universe, this movement is universal."*[96]

Magickal correspondences put the element of Water in the West, which seems appropriate given the persisting tradition that Avalon was once Atlantis.[97] If this is so, then two traditions were to meet in one sacred place. As Alan Richardson points out, *"Those who became initiates of the Sea Mysteries were really seers, pure and simple, whereas the adepts of the Sun-cult were magicians."*[98] And like Avalon, Atlantis is a symbol of lost innocence.

Another mystery begins when attempting to discover the tomb of Arthur. An account by Nennius of Anir, a reputed son of Arthur, has a description of *his* grave which is remarkable.

> *"And when (they) come to measure the mound, they find it sometimes six feet, sometimes nine, sometimes twelve, and sometimes fifteen. Whatever length you find it at one time, you will find it different at another..."*[99]

One is reminded of the stones that reputedly cannot be counted in megalithic circles, such as the Rollrights or those at Stanton Drew.

In 1191, the tomb of Arthur and Guinevere was discovered in the grounds of Glastonbury Abbey. The grave was *"...directly on the extension of Dod Lane...on a spirit or dragon path, where the tomb of a Chinese emperor would have been placed."*[100] A leaden cross inscribed *Rex Arturius* was considered to be conclusive proof of the identity of the royal skeleton and his queen. Thus was the legend established. The sword Excalibur was also found in the grave and given by the bishops to Richard I, who on his way to the Third Crusade, presented the trophy to Scagred of Sicily.

The discovery of Arthur's grave instigated a revival of interest in a figure that seemed to have disappeared with the Dark Ages, an era, according to Morris, *"the worst recorded in the history of Britain."*[101] As Ashe tells us, *"We have no Celtic Homer midway between Arthur and the Romancers, no great sourcebook for the Legend which is similarly close to the Fact."*[102] For their themes, medieval story writers in England turned to the *Matter of Britain*, the only extant history of this country. There, the deeds of King Arthur and the Knights of the Round Table (as the account was now titled) were given great prominence. William of Malmesbury, a Benedictine monk, an order renowned for their scholarship, was Arthur's first chronicler. He was determined, perhaps unlike those who followed him, to establish Arthur as some credible historical figure rather than one who existed only in fable. When writing *Deeds of the Kings of England* in 1125, he described Arthur *"as one who has sustained his tottering country and gave the shattered minds of his fellow citizens an edge for war."*

Geoffrey of Monmouth, another ecclesiastic, whose *History of the Kings of Britain* culminates with Arthur *"...draws on Welsh monastic writing, on Breton folklore...and...is more creative artist than historian; and the realm of Arthur, as known to literature, is his chief creation."*[103] Overseas campaigns and civil rebellion make up the bulk of the story, but Geoffrey's work is important to us because it is the first time Merlin, Avalon, Excalibur, and various named knights are mentioned.[104] Geoffrey wished, like the compilers of *The Mabinogion*, to promote a Welsh Arthur as a symbol of Celtic culture at the expense of the Anglo-Saxons. He succeeded in establishing a separate version, resulting in scholars ever after trying to keep apart (or amalgamate) the two traditions.

Chretien de Troyes, a writer of long verse romances, introduced the theme of courtly love to the tales, and importantly for succeeding tellers of the tales, the relationship between Guinevere and Lancelot, and also Tristram and Iseult. Malory's *Morte d'Arthur* of 1485 established such a definitive English form that the tale was abandoned by continental authors. The Grail as an exclusively Christian symbol makes its first appearance here as does the notion of the "Once and Future King," the notion of the sleeping Arthur surrounded by his knights ready to rise and fight when the nation needs them.[105]

"...King Arthur is not dead, but had by the will of our Lord Jesu into another place; and men say that he shall come again and win the Holy Cross."

Edmund Spenser's rather turgid epic The Faerie Queen:

"...introduces Merlin, Tristram, and other Malory characters; paraphrases a large part of Geoffrey of Monmouth; presents the Tudor dynasty...as the glorious kingdom of the Britons restored, with a suitable pedigree for Elizabeth; and weaves an allegorical linkage between the events and personages of the two periods."[106]

Dryden and Tennyson wrote Arthurian poetry, Purcell produced an opera on the theme, and in the twentieth century, T.H. White wrote the best-selling *The Once and Future King* and Disney made *The Sword in the Stone*. It would be difficult in the twenty-first century to find a place in the world where the Arthurian saga remains unknown, and now it is our purpose to examine some of its elements in detail.

Merlin

Merlin Ambrosius, *Emrys* or *Myrddin,* was a legendary wild man and wizard from Carmarthen, although there is also much to associate him with the North-west of England.[107] He appears to represent the free spirit in man. Cavendish, seeing him as:

> *"Living in harmony with nature and the animals...in touch with... the deep forces of the unconscious mind. Like the wild forest itself, he is an ambivalent being, dangerous but benevolent, sinister but holy."*

While Grigsby adds:

> *"The wolf is no doubt his familiar...he is described as clothed in wolf-skin and bearing a cudgel, which he strikes against the oak trees..."*

Merlin is the offspring of the Thunder God and Cerridwen. He is brother to Olwen who some say is Guinevere. As the guide of Arthur, an affinity with Hermes seems likely, and also Wayland the Smith (after an elf or perhaps the god Volund), as it is Merlin who presents the king with the sword Excalibur, the gift of The Lady of the Lake.[110] Of his feats, revealing the red and white dragons that lay beneath Vortigern's castle and bringing the Giant's Ring from Ireland to construct Stonehenge, go a long way to making Merlin an impressive figure. His Anglo-Saxon name would be *Rof Breoht Woden* (Bright Strength of Woden) and in Elizabethan times, *Robin Goodfellow*. In his earliest incarnation, he is essentially a robust conception of magick.

> *"The wizard himself is both Christian and pre-Christian, a son of the Devil...he evokes the Pagan past."* [111]

A symbol of duality—reason and unreason, known and unknown, order and chaos—in his later incarnation Merlin is more akin to the modern concept of magick, in that he is at one with creation. A meditation by W.E. Butler evokes the magickal persona he later acquires.

> *"I...am also of the race of the Starry Heavens, a spark of that Mighty Flame, and within me also is that Power...I aspire toward that radiant Source of all Power. O thou, the Eternal, whose spark dwells within me, I strive to realise Thee within myself."* [112]

Because of the association with Merlin, a claim is made for Arthur actually dispensing his own wisdom, a little of Merlin's magick rubbing off onto his warrior apprentice perhaps. A tale from the fifteenth or sixteenth century has Arthur uniting *Trystan and Esyllt* (the forerunners of Tristan and Isolde) and ensuring that *March ap Meirchion*, a rival for her affections, "lost Esyllt for good."

A manuscript from the tenth century describes *Some of King Arthur's Wonderful Men*, a splendid collection of fantastical figures, among them Gilla Stag-Leg (*"he would jump three hundred acres at a single jump"*) and *"Sugn the son of Sugnedudd, who would suck up a sea on which there were three hundred ships."* Gwaddn of the Bonfire appears to be the most practical member of the team as *"He would clear the way for Arthur on the march."* Hirsute, Cynyr of the Beautiful Beard, is outdone by Uchdryd Cross-Beard, *"who would throw the bristly red beard which he had across the fifty rafters that were in Arthur's Hall."* Another equally useful figure is Cei who *"because of the extent of his heat...when his companions felt the cold most...would be a means of kindling for them to light a fire..."*

Arthur was a cavalryman (the model of the Medieval *chevalier*) who shrewdly organised the importing of horses and equipped them with armour, as his knights were clad. Being a mounted warrior, he would have been armed with either the Romano-British or the Celtic cavalry sword, a weapon with a greater reach than that of the foot soldier. [113] Any medieval description of his sword Excalibur would have referred to the skills of contemporary swordsmiths.[114] The expertise of such craftsmen was very great, not only in producing fine fighting blades, but in their use of gold and jewels to decorate the hilt and pommel. Some sword makers even engraved their name in the blade.

In the Celtic Cross, Merlin is in the East, the realm of the element Air. In the Tarot, Air is represented by the suit of Swords. Arthur stands in the South, the direction of Fire and in accepting the sword, the two positive or male elements are now linked. In this scheme, the negative elements Water and Earth are given respectively to Nimue (or Vivien), the enchantress who lures Merlin from the path and Morgan, sister of Arthur, and Goddess of Death.[115]

Excalibur has "take me" in runic script on one side of the blade and "cast me away" on the other. When Arthur's sacred task has been fulfilled, the timeless weapon must be returned from whence it came.[116]

The Round Table

It may be that the round table is an evocation of the table of the Last Supper. Cavendish regards this "Grail table" as:

> "...a microcosm...it stands for wholeness, totality, perfection. It is not yet quite perfect though. There is a gap in the circle. One place at the table is empty and the circle will not be complete until the coming of the grail hero." [6117]

Naturally the *number* of places at the table is significant—thirteen—the total of the lunar months and also the number of consonants. "Various mythological companies," as Graves puts it, adopt this number so there may be a leader and twelve followers. Christ among his disciples is the most obvious example of this scheme, as is Odysseus and the Twelve and Arthur and his Knights. William G. Gray explains:

> "The whole point is that only twelve people were humans. They group around the invisible member forming their inner nucleus...a

perfect sphere will need just twelve spheres of its size to cover its surface in equal contact with each other...twelve is a natural harmonic...thirteen being unlucky only applies if the thirteenth person is human, because that would be tantamount to asking the rightful place of God—a risky impertinence for all concerned."

Is the Round Table the wheel of the zodiac with each knight having an astrological sign given to him?[119] Correspondence might be found with the Tarot cards in order from *The Magician* to *The Hanged Man*.[120]

In naming the knights the *Mabinogion*, that collection of tales that often refers to the otherworld, the seasonal cycle, and most importantly the Grail tradition, mentions Bedwyr (Bedivere) and Kei (Kay). Later accounts add Gawain, Perceval, Galahad, Bors, Tristan, and Mordred—but of all, none is so renowned as Lancelot.[121] Chrétien de Troyes tells us:

"No knight was ever born of man and woman, and no knight ever sat in a saddle who was the equal of this man."

Aside from his own exploits, the relationship of Lancelot, Arthur, and Guinevere will forever be remembered for being the most well-known *ménage à trois* of romance.

Arthur's affinity is with the old gods, those of Albion and before. Something of the untamed beast is in his nature, the root of the name *arth* means "bear" or indeed "boar." In an interesting reversal of roles, according to shamanic tradition, it is the bear (Arthur) who advises the shaman (Merlin). In Norse mythology, this animal is sacred to Thor, Odin, and Freya.[122] The presence of the goddess implies a passive female strength as well as the overtly male physicality. The Celts considered the bear to be a lunar creature, so elements of the Moon and Venus are present in its nature. Arthur is also the raven, as is Morrigan the Celtic warrior goddess.[123] Bran, the Irish hero, has the ability to shapeshift into this extraordinary bird, and when Arthur returns, it is said he will assume that form. In *The Dream of Rhonabwy*, a tale in the *Mabinogion*, ravens are depicted as an actual fighting force:

> *"(they) rose full of anger and violence and joy as well, to let the wind into their wings..."*[124]

If Arthur is "the bear," he may be linked with winter and Capricorn,[125] but if his correspondence is with the spring, he may be assigned to Aries.[126] Both Aries and Capricorn are *bestial* signs, horned also, as the unicorn. Does Arthur, as the horned god, magickally give his seed to the grail as he does the unicorn when it "lays its head in the lap of a Virgin"? Before laying aside the question of astrological correspondences, we might suggest that if Arthur was linked with Glastonbury Tor, because of a temple or a stone circle dedicated to the Sun there, then Leo (ruled by the Sun) could be his sign. Hecataeus of Abdera in fourth-century Greece spoke of Britain as *"a magnificent precinct of Apollo."* The ruined church atop the Tor is dedicated to St. Michael, the Christian successor to Mithras.[127] He is also a solar deity, whose symbol (in Persia from where the cult originates) is a lion head surrounded by the rays of the Sun. When Mithras was the recipient of bull sacrifices, *"from its body came vegetation; from its backbone, wheat; and from its blood, wine."* Symbolising the manifestation of great bounty, the bull is associated with beneficent Venus.[128]

Crom, the old agricultural god responsible for ripening the crops, gives a link with the Moon and Venus and the hollow hill (as the Tor is supposed to be) may hold the *sidhe* (pronounced shee)—the fairy folk— "gods but not gods" of whom Crom is one. The female influence at the Tor is personified in St. Bridget (depicted in relief on the west face of the tower) who was said to have been a milk maid.[129]

Beckery at the foot of Wearyall Hill has undoubted associations with the saint.[130] She lived there in 488 AD, staying in a hermitage dedicated to Mary Magdalene. The Salmon of Beckery (the fish shape) or Bride's Mound was once the site of a church dedicated to St. Bridget, and the site of St. Bride's Well is nearby beside the river Brue. *Bridie*, from whom her tradition descends, was the goddess of healing, her festival being Imbolc (February 1st).[131]

Kathy Jones attributes many titles to her[132] including *Mystress of the Underworld* and *Queen of Heaven*, Brigit Morg Ana (*Brigit* the Fiery Arrow, *mor* meaning Great, *Ana* the originating goddess).[133]

Nicholas Mann also assigns *Brigit* to the element of Fire, and as Brigit, Bridie, Bride, and Brighde she is the ancient triple Fire goddess of Ireland and Britain (Brigit's Isles), hence the association with the solar influence of the gods associated with the Tor.[134]

Glastonbury has in recent years played host to the "Cult of the Goddess."

"She is the goddess of the dead Lady of the West. Love, music, beauty, dance fertility, and childbirth are hers. '...those who believed that prehistoric society had been matriarchal and its religion centred upon a Great Goddess, both being destroyed by warlike and patriarchal brutes who had laid the foundation of all the ills of modern society.'"[135]

Of Lancelot's astrological characteristics, we might first mention his supernatural past, him being raised by Vivien (or Niniane), the enchantress and "Lady of the Lake." She is one of three sisters who are the dark counterpart of the three virgins who guard the Grail for the Fisher King.[136] If Lancelot is the alter ego of Gawain, the "Hawk of May" (Taurus), we may assign Lancelot to the opposite month, November, so he falls under the sign of Scorpio.[137] Lancelot has a castle in Northumberland, celebrated for its dragon legends—the dragon being a symbol of Scorpio. The dragon is also the enemy of solar deities, their struggle being between that of light and dark. The relationship is symbiotic, providing the tension needed to continue the cycle of growth and decay. Jung considered that:

"...the slaying of the dragon symbolised...the emergence of a strong independent ego...from out of a state of...unconsciousness."[138]

The solar cult that followed the matriarchal age wished to eradicate the female element, preferring earthly mortality (male) to heavenly immortality (female). Much destruction of female monsters abounds in the myths; the snake Pythia is disposed of by Apollo and Perseus accounts for the Medusa. The medieval persecution of witches is the horrific outcome of such thinking. The trend is only reversed when the alchemists restore sympathetic magick in Tudor times.

An incisive delineation of the character of Lancelot is provided by Alan Richardson. For him, the knight has:

> "*...a brooding sort of compassion; a grave kind of sympathy; the grizzled heart of a simple man made wise by a lifetime of battles, both within and without. There are hints of darkness, flashes of cruelty, and a capacity for ruthlessness as a last resort.*"[139]

In Arthur and Lancelot, two overtly male figures possess an equally strong magickal or passive side to their nature and both can be seen as the personification of a sacrificial god. The legend of the sacrificial king has been cited as the motive for the death of several notable figures of history. King William II (William Rufus), Thomas Becket, and Joan of Arc may well have been voluntary victims of sacrifice.[140] Arthur, who in the guise of a boar (spring—and fertility) slays winter in the personification of Tammuz the Sumerian deity, and (then as Adonis) is slain by a boar himself. Shakespeare's Richard III (V ii ll. 7-11) assigns the wild boar to Richard, and in the person of the god, he gores England, bringing sterility to the country and turning it into The Waste Land.

> "*The wretched, bloody and usurping boar,*
> *That spoil'd your summer fields and fruitful vines,*
> *Swills your warm blood like wash, and makes his trough*
> *In your embowell'd bosoms—this foul swine,*
> *Is now even in the centre of this isle...*"

The death of Adonis/Arthur is a sacrifice to Aphrodite his lover, perhaps incarnated in the person of Guinevere.[141] United in their divine love for this earthly manifestation of the eternal woman, Arthur and Lancelot are at once brothers in arms and foes. The queen is no vapid vamp; she is a learned yet essentially human figure with much of the innocence of the St. Bridget about her. One should also take into account the practical side of love and lust in these times.

To be "bedded" meant warmth and companionship, being rejected—
isolation and loneliness. This excerpt from the Anglo-Saxon elegy,
The Wife's Lament, starkly depicts the outcome of a cruel parting
between a loving couple:

> *"...There are lovers on earth,*
> *Lovers alive who lie in bed,*
> *When I pass through this earth-cave alone*
> *and out under the oak tree at dawn;*
> *there I must sit through the long summer's day*
> *and there I mourn my miseries..."[142]*

Intimate details of Arthur's relationship with his queen are
impossible to find in any of the existing texts. Paradoxically, those same
references reveal Lancelot constantly admitting the deepest of feelings
for Guinevere. His is *"the path of the warrior who chooses his queen, the
archetypal woman..."* and in Guinevere (the Welsh *Gwenhwyfar* means
"White Phantom"), he sees purity and self-sacrifice, qualities he owns
himself.[143] Guinevere is constantly dressed in white as if to promote her
innocence and show her distance from the situation in which she finds
herself. Given that later in the story, she would have perished at the
stake had not Lancelot rescued her, perhaps he is the saviour of both
the body and soul of the queen. Lancelot never can espouse illusion and
ultimately he chooses to see Guinevere's innocence as a mortal proof
of the divine workings of the cosmos. Yet an inner conflict is always
present for Lancelot in his dual role as Guinevere's champion (and lover)
and the necessity for him to own.

Guinevere evokes Arthur's jealousy on another occasion when
Yder (like Gwynn, another son of Nudd) rescues her from a bear.
Guinevere's later announcement—that she would have preferred Yder
or the bear as her lover rather than Arthur—seems a trifle tactless.
Arthur's reaction is to send the young man off to the Mount of Frogs
(Brent Knoll) to fight the giants (or dragons) residing there. Yder
succeeds in killing them but loses his life in doing so. In penance for
causing Yder's death, Arthur gives the land around Brent Knoll to
the monks of Glastonbury.

Morgan le Fay (perhaps Morrigan) is Arthur's half-sister with whom he may have had an incestuous relationship. "Fay" (Fairy) refers to an other-worldly figure:

> "...*tall, commanding and seductively beautiful. Dominating, ruthless, sensual and unpredictable...sometimes benevolent...sometimes cruel...(with) formidable magical powers...*"[144]

One who, in this event, plots against Arthur and betrays him on every possible occasion. She attempts to steal Excalibur, thus robbing the hero of his greatest asset. Richard Cavendish explains the *leitmotif* that accompanies such an enchantress in the romances.

> "...*a hero in danger from an enchantress, who desires him, hates him, or both...is related to the old and widespread theme of the evilness of woman, which is linked with her sexual allure. The enchantress wants either to kill the hero...or more often to do away with him metaphorically by keeping him prisoner in her own realm, so preventing him from pursuing his own career in the world. She entangles him in a web of mindless sensual pleasure, in which he loses his capacity for action. The encounter with the femme fatale is one of the perils which the true hero must experience and survive.*"[145]

Morgan le Fay was, ironically perhaps, once the pupil of Merlin and often perceived as the dark alter-ego of Guinevere, mainly due to Malory's description of her as "a clerk of necromancy." Geoffrey of Monmouth does not ascribe sorcery to Morgan, merely noting that, *"She...knows an art by which to change her shape, and to cleave the air on new wings like Daedalus."* She brings Arthur to Avalon (seen as the realm of King Avallach, perhaps Morgan's father) when he is dying. With her nine maidens (or *Morgens*) Morgan nurses the king.[146] Because of her association with the end of Arthur, she is seen as the bringer of Death. As Yeats has it, *"What else can death be but the beginning of wisdom and power and beauty?"* By being so covert, Morgan seems strangely distant from her powers. Yeats' insight is again appropriate: "If I had her power of vision, I would know all the wisdom of the gods, and her visions do not interest her."[147]

In regarding this particular reference to death, we might return briefly to Lancelot's affinity with the astrological sign of Scorpio and its attendant associations with death. Arthur, being Aries, the two are united by the traditional planetary ruler of their signs, Mars, associated with war and the sexual urge. Of Scorpio, astrologer Fred Gettings has more to add:

> *"Some astrologers insist that the eagle was used in ancient times to stand in place of Scorpio itself...the rationale seems to be that since Scorpio is the sign in which redemption takes place, then it alone of all the twelve signs of the zodiac may be represented by two images. The image of the scorpion represents the unredeemed nature, while the image of the aspiring eagle symbolises the redeemed nature. The esoteric theories underlying such astrological doctrine appear to support this view, which is actually expressed in imagery of Dante."[148]*

Aries is associated with the primal energy, that of life, thus we have Life and Death side by side. A correspondence with the Tarot gives us the Arcana of The Emperor and Death. On a mundane level, Scorpio does have a strong affinity with Aries because above all, Scorpio cannot bear deceit. At their most virtuous, the native Arian manifests only an honesty that cannot be questioned. Death has its mystery, though perhaps tempered by being the only certainty we can claim in our earthly lives.

> *"'Death is our eternal companion,' Don Juan said with a most serious air. 'It is always to our left at an arm's length.'"[149]*

Death, war, sacrifice—the bloody elements that are contained in the Arthurian legend. It is small wonder that those who subsequently made Christianity an intrinsic part of the legend altered and refashioned it for their own ends.

Pagan Hero or Christian King?

Even if Joseph of Arimathea, accompanied by the Christ-child, did not visit Glastonbury (or Priddy) in Somerset, a Christian settlement was established there early in its history. A more permanent monument to the faith was the "Old Church" at the summit of the Tor which William of Malmesbury considered to have been built in 180 AD. The Abbey found great favour among the rulers of Wessex in the tenth century and successfully resisted the attempts by the bishops in nearby Wells to rob Glastonbury of its independence. This they attempted to do by force and Ponter's Ball (the Bridge Perilous) was constructed, not as a sacred enclosure (as archaeologist Ralegh Radford insisted), but as a defensive earthwork to deter the *"armed bands (who) were sent from Wells to take Glastonbury by force and punish its monks... "[150]*

By the Middle Ages, the Abbey was established as the sacred centre of Wessex, if not England. One abbot, Richard Beere:

> *"...was very anxious to promote the cult of Joseph of Arimathea and had made a new crypt beneath Lady Chapel of the abbey, reputedly the site of the wattle church, as a shrine to the saint."[151]*

On a visit with a companion to the Abbey in 2001, this writer could have been found meditating at the altar in that same crypt and being immediately aware of an energy that was not transcendental Christian, but pure magick.[152] The image of the Tarot *Magician* filled his consciousness so overwhelmingly that the symbols of the four suits filled the altar before him. The vision is perhaps not so surprising, as Dion Fortune who lived in Glastonbury in the 1920s confirmed.[153] She believed that neither Paganism nor Christianity held the monopoly of belief in Glastonbury, a view that shapes any understanding of the very tangible power surrounding this singular Somerset market town.[154]

Frederick Bligh Bond, a Bristolian engineer who directed the excavations at Glastonbury Abbey in the 1920s believed that:

> *"Glastonbury lay under the special protection of a body of elevated souls...and that the sacred and esoteric science of gematria (holy numbers) underpinned the planning of the abbey."[155]*

This extraordinary figure is primarily remembered for blotting his copybook with the ecclesiastical establishment when he revealed that he had been aided by supernatural forces when he determined the site of the original Abbey buildings. His amanuensis, a medieval monk, supposedly gave Bligh Bond an extravagant description of Arthur's tomb.

"...over Arthur's tombe to the Est window it was fayrer and muchy gilt soe that the lightes of the Altar shold shine thereon and make a glory."[156]

The monument, before it was destroyed during the Reformation, would have been an impressive sight, as Ronald Hutton imagines.

"A black marble tomb with a lion at each corner and an effigy of a king at its foot...Beyond was the high altar, with a silver and gilt antependium set before it. In front of it also were three shrines containing the relics of the saints."[157]

It is evident that Arthur is being commemorated as a national hero—even more, a symbol of England and the English, as Dion Fortune puts it, *"a myth, which is by its nature in harmony with our national tradition."*[158] From the Black Prince to Wellington, from Drake to Churchill, the history of our country resounds with the acclaim awarded the hero, particularly when his victory is against all odds. When "fortune favours the bold" in great measure, the reward might be immortality. Even Harold Godwin, though defeated at Hastings dies with his reputation intact, sacrificing himself in defense of the realm. Cromwell may have brought a monarch to the block, but the notion of Kings ruling by divine right has not been eliminated entirely from our national consciousness. The Secret of the Golden Flower, a book of Chinese Yoga, describes:

"...when the Light circulates, the powers of the whole body arrange themselves before its throne, just when the holy king has taken possession of the capital and has laid down the fundamental rules of order, all the states approach with tribute...Therefore you only have to make the Light circulate; that is the deepest and most wonderful secret."[159]

Rex Quondam, Rex Futurus, means that the king will return in England's hour of need. Does Arthur personify England as William Blake and later G.K. Chesterton believed? If Albion is a gigantic representation of our land (a *Titan*, the gods that ruled before the coming of Zeus and the rest) then as Blake says, *"The stories of Arthur are the acts of Albion, applied to a Prince of the fifth century."*

In 1940, Dion Fortune believed she could ward off the threat of a Nazi invasion. In those times, Winston Churchill, the war leader, made much of "defending our heritage." Fortune was a great admirer of "Mr. Churchill," as she always referred to him, and defending the actual earth of England would have appealed strongly to her. The landscape of Somerset particularly appealed to her, and she set her magickal novel *The Sea Priestess* there. *"The Old Gods guard their ground,"* she believed. It was perhaps obvious that she would turn to Avalon for supernatural aid as her contribution to the war effort.

> *"Here the veil that hides the Unseen is thin...the souls of men may come and go between the inner and outer planes."*[160]

It is said that Arthur lies asleep in Camelot (Cadbury Camp), but it was within the depths of Glastonbury Tor where Dion Fortune sought and found:

> *"...three rays of light...forming themselves into a triangle. One side was coloured red; this was associated with King Arthur. Another side was coloured blue and linked with Merlin. While the third side, the purple side, was governed by...the Master Jesus."*[161]

Later, the Virgin Mary was added to this august company. Dion Fortune cast herself in the role of the Grail bearer and worked her magick, which she always described as *"the art of causing changes in consciousness."* Whether the efforts of Fortune successfully turned the tide of the war is debatable, but her actions seem in line with the tremendous power of belief that existed in England at the beginning of the war, perhaps epitomised by the famous minute of prayer that followed the nine o'clock news every night and was inaugurated by Wellesley Tudor-Pole.

A portal in the Tor leading to another realm originates with the belief that within lies the kingdom of Gwynn ap Nudd. Nicholas Mann suggests that this entrance way into the Tor may be through tunnels from the Abbey.[162] Access (through White Spring cave) seems only to be possible at certain times of the year, such as at Samhain (Nov. 1st) when the geophysical energies within the mound are intensified by the action of the White Spring and Red Spring and the spirits of the place are aroused. The dragon energy that is also associated with the place can be stimulated by walking the labyrinth, the sacred paths around the Tor.

Arthur may also represent that catalyst of change that acts upon all societies, his spiritual strength becoming a political force, so his essence is in Robespierre or Marx, men who saw themselves as the catalyst of social change. In the twentieth century, Hitler yearned for the return of Charlemagne, Gandhi, and the resurgence of the old India, and even now Israel still desires the repossession of Zion. It had been Shelley who had championed a free society:

> *"The painted veil, by those who were, called life,*
> *Which mimicked, as with colours idly spread,*
> *All men believed or hoped, is torn aside;*
> *The loathsome mask has fallen, the man remains*
> *Sceptreless, free, uncircumscribed, but man..."*

Jean Jaures encourages us to *"take from the altars of the past the fire, not the ashes,"* and perhaps it can be said that even the New Age has within it both the spirit of Arthur and Merlin. Blake desired a new Jerusalem, and modern man wants a new Earth.

So, we must conclude that Arthur has become, whether we like it or not, a symbol of many things. It might be one of modern magick, so that:

> *"...the tales within the Arthurian Cycle contain fragments of occult lore of incredible age, and that Arthur, Morgan le Fay and the rest were hereditary initiatic titles rather than specific historical personages."*[163]

Arthur too may be the potent representation of a golden age where Camelot is seen as the secure citadel within a perfect world.

As Ashe puts it, *"The visionary kingdom stands, unshaken by time, with the power and immortality of the imagination."* And this Shangri-La could be a myth from the Minoan-Mycenean world transposed to Britain. The story of Arthur is a paradox, and as Castaneda reminds us, *"...only if one pits two views against each other can one weasel between them to arrive at the real world."* It is fitting that William G. Gray, who knew much about archetypes, should pose our concluding question concerning *the image* of Arthur.

> *"We have to ask ourselves what is so important about any image or symbol that it continues to stir human consciousness centuries its exact origins have faded into oblivion...Whatever speaks to us now from our past at all, has still something of value to tell us now and for the future."[166]*

The Waste Land

The Waste Land is a term used by Chretien de Troyes to describe a land empty of spiritual worth. It is also the title of a celebrated poem by T.S. Eliot, written a few years after the First World War. The bringing of fertility and the *"restoring of the rivers to their channels"* is the underlying theme of the work, though renowned for being overlaid with numerous other references.[167] When did the universal consciousness go through a sudden and vigorous change making ripples that extended into the heart of the twentieth century? On the 23rd of March 1922, Franz Kafka reflected in his diary his own misgivings and those of his generation about the future, writing of, *"The perpetually shifting frontier that lies between ordinary life and the terror that would seem to be real."[168]* In that same year, the Russian Civil War—the bloody sequel to the 1917 revolution—raged and the Irish Free State, the result of another civil conflict, was inaugurated. The BBC was given its charter by the government, and women were permitted to practise as solicitors. Several works, later to be regarded as literary milestones, were published in 1922—*Ulysses* by James Joyce, *The Golden Bough* by Sir

James Frazer, *Siddhartha* by Herman Hesse, and *The Beautiful and the Damned* by Scott Fitzgerald. Marcel Proust died, and fittingly, a trio of writers who would later represent a new wave—Jack Kerouac, Kingsley Amis, and Philip Larkin—were born.

For poets, the most significant event was the publication of *The Waste Land.* Like *Ulysses,* it was seen by many as an incredible creative achievement.[169] The gestation of the poem is well-documented, particularly Eliot's nervous collapse and his journeying to Switzerland where he worked on a long poem first begun in 1919. This, after drastic pruning at the hands of fellow poet Ezra Pound, subsequently became *The Waste Land.* Seen as the first modernist poem and rightly so, it is in tune with its time, iconoclastic, multi-layered, and echoing the structures and rhythms of jazz. A generation saw within it a great deal that it felt ought to be said, and how that generation wanted to perceive the world—as a diverse and paradoxical whole. In Evelyn Waugh's *Brideshead Revisited,* the chapter that so memorably evokes 1920s Oxford features a scene where Anthony Blanche *"recited passages from The Waste Land to the sweatered and muffled throng on its way to the river."* The intelligentsia saw Eliot as one of a company that included Einstein and Picasso. Interestingly, Eliot mentions the scientist but not the artist in his 1923 essay, *Ulysses, Order, and Myth.*[170] In the same piece is a phrase that ostensibly refers to *Ulysses* but might equally well be a description of Eliot's own work *"...it has given me all the surprise, delight and terror that I can require..."* After a nod of acknowledgment towards Wyndham Lewis and W.B. Yeats, Eliot ends by proposing that *"Instead of narrative method, we may now use the mythical method."*

In *The Idea of a Christian Society,* another essay from the same volume, Eliot reveals his affinity with the transcendental.[171] "It may be observed that the natural life and the supernatural life have a conformity with each other which neither has with the mechanistic life..." He follows this with the telling prediction that:

"We are being made aware that the organization of society on the principle of private profit, as well as public destruction, is leading

both to the deformation of humanity by unregulated industrialism,
and to the exhaustion of natural resources, and that a good deal of
our material progress is a progress for which succeeding generations
may have to pay dearly."[172]

Nearly a century later, many are wondering whether such timely warnings have been heeded too late. A fascinating and elusive character, sensitive to the point of being in constant mental anguish, Thomas Stearns Eliot, deliberately or not, shrank from much human contact.[173] His relationship with his parents was troubled; his marriage to a wife who gradually became insane, a source of despair. An American born in St. Louis, Missouri in 1888, Eliot quickly became an Anglophile and a great lover of all things European, as did many of his literary contemporaries. Once established, he became a literary lion and perhaps due to his American sensibility, brought an original vision to the world of English letters. Though a publisher, editor, and speaker as well as a poet, Eliot was no dry intellectual, having a fine wit and a delectation for drink. His rigorous obeisance to the dictates of convention disguised a vigorous inner self. He was open to the influences of the supernatural, and in 1920, took part in séances organised by Ouspensky. Gilbert Seldes, in a review of *The Waste Land* written not long after its publication, compares Eliot's character to the French poet Jules Laforgue:

"His natural genius was made up of sensibility, irony, imagination,
and clairvoyance; he chose to nourish it with positive knowledge
(connaisance positives), with all philosophies and all literatures..."[174]

In the same collection, F.O. Matthiessen mentions the Henry James essay "The Art of Fiction" an excellent evocation of a writer's working method. James' view, applied to Eliot's transcendental predilections, is strangely apposite.

"The power to guess the unseen from the seen, to trace the implication
of things, to judge the whole piece by the pattern, the condition of
feeling life, in general, so completely that you are well on your way
to knowing any particular corner of it..."[175]

Eliot's intriguing statement in his *The Use of Poetry and the Use of Criticism* that, *"I myself should like an audience which could neither read nor write"* is examined by C.K. Stead.

> *"...he (Eliot) argued that poetry could communicate even before it was understood. In this way he was acknowledging that the experience of poetry is foremost an aural, emotional experience, one which approximates of listening to music..."*[176]

The *Waste Land* is certainly a *meisterwerk*, the catalyst for ten thousand theses, a cornucopia of references for the scholar. One hundred and forty-seven quotations are embedded in the text, taken from sources as far-ranging as *The Bible* and Swinburne. References to Frazer's *Golden Bough*, Jessie L. Weston's *From Ritual to Romance*, the Grail legend, the Tarot, the Upanishads, and the Buddhist *Book of the Dead*. Like Joyce, Eliot was acutely aware that he was doing something new. Virginia Woolf, when referring to their own literary generation, said *"We're not as good as Keats."* Eliot had responded by saying *"Yes we are...we're trying to do something harder."*[178]

Eliot's decrying of materialism and a yearning for transcendence resonates with a deep echo in our own times. In the 1920s, *The Waste Land* was seen as a *cri de coeur* of a disaffected youth, but, as Bob Dylan would do a couple of generations later, Eliot eschewed the role of "spokesman for a generation." With an enigmatic piece *Thoughts after Lambeth*, written in 1931, Eliot qualified his opinion of his most celebrated poem.

> *"...some of the more approving critics said I had expressed the 'disillusionment of a generation,' which is nonsense. I may have expressed for them their own disillusion of being disillusioned..."*[179]

Eliot was convinced that the poet should be a medium for the lyrical or enlightening experience; neither would he have separated these two qualities. His attitude to artistic purpose is the same as that of a magician's *raison d'être*.

> "...*a continual surrender of himself [the poet] as he is at the moment to something which is more valuable. The progress of an artist is a continual self-sacrifice, a continual extinction of personality...*"[180]

Eliot had an acute sense of "the Void," and although he would have been familiar with the Buddhist conception, to him it was being conscious of one's life *"drained of inner significance and meaning."*[181] One might conclude, as does his biographer Peter Ackroyd, that he had, *"a clairvoyant sense of his time—because he found its preoccupations within himself."*[182] Yet, like Plato, Eliot was no lover of democracy. He had an almost evangelical desire to enlighten and inform that part of society he would have referred to as "the masses" and tried his best to do so.[183] Eliot was almost a spiritual and intellectual messiah, one perhaps divorced from common experience so that *"...reality lay only within himself, to be explored in prayer, meditation and in his own creative work."*[184]

It was Eliot's wish to be buried in East Coker in Somerset[185] and he may have had a secret affection for Wessex[186] like his fellow American and literary figure Steinbeck, who took a house near South Cadbury. The transatlantic affection for things mythical and Arthurian seems to grow and grow. One might end with Eliot's line from his poem *East Coker. "In my beginning is my end."* The endless cycle is a theme personified in the next section, a view of one of the major themes of *The Waste Land*—The Quest for the Holy Grail.

Cauldron or Chalice?

The metaphysical aspect of the Grail has been discussed in some detail within the pages of *Clown and Chalice*, a work by this writer, so it would be pointless to cover again the same ground. As it is a major theme in any Arthurian study, an understanding of its supposed origin and nature is essential, particularly with regard to its powers.

> *"The Grail provided the power to solve every spiritual problem mankind would ever have.*

A little later this concept came out on a somewhat lower scale as the 'Stone' of the Alchemists."[187]

Arthur has been depicted holding Excalibur in his right hand, the Grail in his left. How has he obtained the sacred vessel? Did he steal it? The question is not so strange as it appears, for, *"The theft of the cauldron is a theme that appears again and again in Indian myth..."*[188]

In ancient tales, securing the sacred treasure, be it Cauldron or Grail, is assigned to the hero.[189] In the later tradition, it is only the pure of heart who may encounter it. Arthur, being of hero stock, features in a Welsh tale *The Spoils of Annwfn*, which tells of him securing a cauldron of plenty from the chief of Annwfn who may be Gwnn or Gwyn the son of Nudd and king of the Otherworld.[190] Some tales even identify Arthur with Gwyn, who gives the prefix *Win* to many English towns, significantly Winchester, the supposed location of the Round Table.

The cauldron of Cerridwen, a pre-Christian symbol of the female, which bestowed renewal, transformation, and plenty is the womb of the Great Goddess—Demeter and Isis.[191] Cerridwen herself is the Celtic symbol of inspiration, wisdom, and justice, and it is significant that the concept of "justice" appears to be intrinsically female. We have come to associate "the Law," or more specifically the "Books of the Law" with the male predilection for reason and order (the left brain), but this was not always so. The Tarot card *Justice* depicts a female figure who does not act but *reacts*, and in doing so, retains the principle of *equilibrium*. Like *The High Priestess* who sits between the pillars of *Jachin* (Will) and *Boaz* (Providence), her role is to re-establish the balance between the individual and the universal. We have conscious choice—that is, free will—and it is our *conscience* that should always be appealed to for it *unconsciously* makes the right decision. It does so in accord with the universe and reflects the freedom gained by man when he embraces the will of heaven. It might be possible to gain wisdom through the melding of the conscious and sub-conscious mind (what Jung calls *"self-division"*), a return to a time when *"the land of the mortals and the land of the gods were joined and man could commune with his ancestors..."*[192]

The knowledge that the Grail bestows may also be the realisation that existence is both temporal and eternal. Stanislav Grof speaks of:

"People who have during their lifetime experientially confronted birth and death and connected with the transpersonal dimension (and) have good reason to believe that their physical demise will not mean the end of their existence."[193]

It seems that the artefact, be it Grail, cauldron, or stone is a catalyst for enlightenment. Man has always been interested in possessing solutions to the mysteries of the universe. Charles Williams, the author of *War in Heaven* (a novel about the Grail), wrote a sequel titled *Many Dimensions* in which:

"Natural and divine law are represented by the Stone (once set in the crown of King Solomon) which is here the object of the quest. This stone will work miracles. By its aid, the categories of Time and Space can be transcended." [194]

The anthropomorphic stage of transmutation to the Ciborium (Eucharistic emblem) is the Salmon of Wisdom.[195] Because the vessel is used for wine and the ritual linked with bread, this is seen as a development from animal to vegetable sacrifice. The theme of sacrifice is personified in the Fisher King, the guardian of the Grail.[196] This always ailing figure is essential to the legend, though always depicted as if in a mist. He may even be King Arthur before the Grail is restored to him, making him whole. Jeffrey Gantz, in an introduction to his translation of *The Mabinogion*, supports Eschenbach's view that:

"...the Fisher King has been sexually incapacitated by a poisoned-spear thrust (and demonstrates) Crestien's...connection between ailing king and wasteland. This idea of the sympathetic relationship between the potency of the king and the fertility of the land is supported by Irish texts which hint that a king might be ritually married to the tutelary earth goddess of the tribe."[197]

His wound is known as the "dolorous stroke" and according to Mallory, it is *Pellean, the Fisher King* who receives this "dolorous stroke" from Balin le Sauvage. As soon as this happens, *"the castle walls collapse, the crops fail, and the trees lose their leaves."*[198] A similarly symbolic blow occurs in other traditions, such as when Shiva is attacked by the sages who, *"...castrate him...unaware of who he is, thinking him a simple madman. But the wound...has dreadful consequences."*[199] When Adonis is gored by a boar, the land suffers too. Such myths may simply be the seasonal round depicted in microcosm, for in winter, the seed lies dormant (The Fisher King) waiting for the spring (the Grail) and the renewal of life. There may even be a link with the cold, lifeless nature of the Moon, being seen as impotent—like the Fisher King.[200] This very same impotence (or mental/spiritual incapacity) on the part of Percival leads him to be unable to complete the Quest.[201]

*"When you went to the court of the lame king and saw...marvels...
you asked neither their cause not their meaning. Had you asked, the
king would have been made well and the kingdom made peaceful..."*[202]

Words spoken by the loathsome apparition that may be Morrigan and a Grail maiden at the same time, simultaneously the creator and destroyer in the great tradition of a powerful goddess. Perhaps the Grail yearns to be entered by the lance to successfully bring about its flowering. F. O. Matthiessen mentions the view of Jessie L. Weston:

*"...the researches of psychology (that) pointed to the close union
in all these myths of the physical and the spiritual, to the fact that
their symbolism was basically sexual—in the Cup and the Lance of
the Grail legend as well as the Orpheus cults; pointed, in brief to the
fundamental relation between the well-springs of sex and religion."*[203]

As to the physical existence of an object which is the Grail, as we know, this has been the *raison d'être* of many a wild goose chase in recent years.[204] Glastonbury Abbey never actually laid claim to possessing the Grail, though it did:

*"...possess numerous relics of the Passion, including several pieces of
the cross, some of the earth in which the cross stood, a thorn from the
crown of thorns, and part of the table of the last supper."*[205]

Of its final resting place, *"and beyond this, Sarras the Land of the Trinity, to which the Grail finally departs."*[206] This may be the Eden that Blake insists upon.[207] We might conclude that the *search is paramount, not the attainment* as in any spiritual exercise. As William G. Gray has it:

> *"It is the questing itself which is important, the constant search for something just beyond immediate reach...Constantly achieving the idea, yet never the actuality it indicates..."*[208]

Also of extreme importance is the manner in which enlightenment is attained, and the initiate's journey into the unknown is at the very heart of all traditions of magick. William G. Gray is as always pragmatic:

> *"...we have to experience hell in order to handle heaven. Humans have to be subjected to traumatic experiences which are sufficiently strong enough to alter their essential selves into entirely different types of being before they become able to deal with what might be called Divine conditions of consciousness...(leading to) the soul (living) in a condition wherein everything seemed to consist of sheer light-energy."*[209]

The actual encounter with our own "shadow," as Jung would describe it, is on the Quest, as on all spiritual journeys, personified by the:

> *"'Dweller on the Threshold' who guarded the gates of the ancient Mysteries. This fabled horror represents everything in ourselves that seeks to prevent us from achieving a state of spiritual perfection. Either we challenge and conquer this negative side of our nature, or we remain an outsider and get no closer consciously, to the truth of our Inner Identities."* [210]

In the twenty-first century, we naturally believe that we have successfully eradicated all impediments to liberality, yet this is not a superficial cleansing that is being considered. This goes to the very heart of our individual and, by definition, the universal mind.

> *"Repression...is a process by which the personality protects itself against distasteful concepts. By thrusting them without the*

horizon of consciousness into the dark and forbidding region of the Unconscious." [211]

The secret of the Grail lies in the Somerset landscape.[212] In the Quest, *"the knights of Arthur on the quest of the Graal, spent the last night of their pilgrimage in a chapel"*[213] at Pons Perilis, now a meeting of roads, once an ancient river crossing. Here was to be the final before a short stretch led them to be soon acquainted with the Grail. This place might be the river Styx in another tradition, for:

"...it was not the dangers of a river crossing that made this spot feared, but the spiritual terrors that here beset the questing soul on the final stage of the Quest journey. Here the Knights of the Graal watched all night until early the next morning when they might pass to the holy earth of Avalon, to be greeted by the Fisher King and shown the Graal with its guard of virgins within Chalice Hill. And some died of bliss at the sight, and none ever walked with men the same again."[215]

William of Malmsebury and John of Glastonbury both wrote that St. Bridget visited Glastonbury in 488 AD and occupied an oratory at Beckery dedicated to Mary Magdalene.[216] Another Mary features when:

"...King Arthur was believed to have received a crystal cross at the hands of Our Lady—the cross he emblazoned on his shield and banner; the cross which later was cut by the abbots of Glastonbury on their great seal."[217]

The nature of the gift is not what is important, but the avowal of creation to share her bounty. As Don Juan tells Castaneda, *"A warrior is always joyful because his love...the earth, embraces him and bestows upon him inconceivable gifts."*[218] The ultimate gift will be the Grail, but not in the form that we envisage it.[218] As William G. Gray explains:

"Nowhere was the Grail known as a cup, but specifically a Vessel, which could be a container of any kind. It was the principle of containment that was signified, and the Blood-Royal was always considered as a very special inheritance handed down genetically

from the earliest times to our days, which was said to confer kingly characteristics on those who bore even the slightest trace of it."[220]

The search inside oneself is the true nature of the quest, for the truths discovered there are the most relevant and valuable to the individual. It may be that the *anima* in man responds more powerfully to the feminine nature residing in the Grail. Dante imagines that an intercession from the Virgin bestows a mystical insight into the nature of the Trinity and the Incarnation. It seems that this feminine aspect is believed to hold the key to wisdom, for as W.B. Yeats remarked, "... *women come more easily than men to that wisdom which ancient peoples... think the only wisdom.*" Before the cult of the Virgin was, of course, the cult of the goddess. Originally, the goddess went by a number of names, in Crete she is Rhea, in Gozo—Calypso, Atlas' daughter. She is also Venus or Aphrodite who sprang from sea foam. Athene, who sprang from elsewhere, namely the forehead of Zeus, may too have been part of the same school. Tacitus, in *Germania* describes:

> "...*the days of rejoicing and merrymaking...No one goes to war, no one takes up arms; every iron object is locked away. Then, and only then, are peace and quiet known and welcomed...*"

But as we enter the New Age, do its adherents realise the true nature of the Goddess and indeed, her original purpose. William G. Gray explains that those we regard as primitive people:

> "...*were matriarchally minded. For them, the Mother Archetype was a universal producer and provider, but great as she was, her gifts had to be taken the hard way in most cases. Mothers could be cruel or kind, and she was certainly both. Being female, mothers loved strong sons... and when they died She would replace them in Her womb and bring them back to life again...Resurrection was a simple as that.*"[222]

To quote Alan Richardson, "...*And to cling to any spiritual experience is to create a tyranny for ourselves.*" For we must advance always, with a glance at the past and what it may teach us, but with our eyes, scanning the present and ready for the future.

Ancient & Modern

The vexing question in all this, is "When did the New Age begin?" or "Has the New Age begun?" or even "Is the New Age over?" Some associate the New Age with the coming of the Age of Aquarius, but opinions even differ as to the precise date of that event.

Does the Industrial Revolution usher in that age or the beginning of the twentieth century? Whatever the answer, the New Age is with us. The difficulty, then, is to define what it means to be part of it.

To anyone who knew the 1960s, the New Age might merely seem to be the continuation of a well-established theme. Similarities can rapidly be made to disappear with the evocation, "that was then, and this is now." It is always difficult to assess any era in history dispassionately, let alone accurately, even though those who lived in that time may still be alive. Even the greatest of our historians often struggle to present a true picture of time. For instance, views of late 1960s culture range from the revisionist style of an Austin Powers movie to exhaustive studies of socialist machinations. As always, the truth lies somewhere in between. The values of the 1960s were famously condemned by Margaret Thatcher when she was Prime Minister, and it is with hindsight difficult to view wholesale drug taking and promiscuity as anything but hedonistic and irresponsible. Hallucinogens were touted as instant enlightenment, prompting George Harrison to offer the suitably enigmatic comment:

"You can't say LSD is good or bad because it's good AND bad. It's both of them and neither of them all together."[223]

Any assessment of the "Swinging Sixties" fails if it isolates any one part of the scene and believes that to be the whole, for that culture was woven of many threads, each with its own agenda, though they may have been interdependent. Depending on where you stood, the zeitgeist would appear in a different light. Many, such as this writer, began the decade as a schoolboy and left it with a degree. A family struggling to make ends meet while they lived in a council house in Saltford would not necessarily view the landscape through a pair of psychedelic glasses.

The 1960s heralded enormous change, the more so because there was no hint from what had gone before as to the nature of what would follow. It was the very magnitude of that upheaval that shocked and frightened an older generation. Poor things, they were not prepared. To be there and watching that particular dawn was a wondrous sight that can never be recreated, no matter how much every detail is logged or every nook and cranny scoured for hidden meaning. Spiritual and intellectual growth flourished at an alarming rate, and for those prepared to embrace it, a *"splendid time was guaranteed for all."* As Ken Kesey remembered:

> *"Suddenly people were stripped before one another and behold: we were beautiful. Naked and helpless and sensitive as a snake after skinning but far more human..."*[224]

The establishment did not care for much of it, and their reactions ranged from puzzled amusement to overt hostility. In England, used as we were to eccentricity, the meeting of new and old did not lead to as much confrontation as was later to happen, often tragically, in America. There, the stage was decked with politics and compromise did not seem possible, so many drowned in a tide of ignorance and bigotry. In many ways, the template was cut for the New Age, but before that, the door that had been so very determinedly opened was gently but irretrievably closed once more. Of that door Ron Thelin, a San Francisco activist, reflected:

> *"(It) was blown open by God, and light shone in on the world, huge amounts of light, at first blinding...there's still a light under the door...(it) can always be opened again."*[225]

And somehow, kept ajar it was...

A New Meaning

Written in 1992, the preface to *Llewellyn's New Age Series* of "occult" and "magick" books came as close as anything to a definition of The New Age. The most relevant sentiment seems to be:

> *"...it's a major change in consciousness found within each of us as we learn to bring forth and manifest powers that humanity has always potentially had..."*

The term *New Age* (or New Era) has certainly been used before. Alice Bailey used it in reference to the transition from the age of Pisces to that of Aquarius, and it is likely that thinkers at the beginning of the twentieth century spoke of the coming century in those terms. In naming those who were definite progenitors of the New Age it is almost impossible to be totally inclusive, but Edgar Cayce, Nicholas Roerich, and Rudolf Steiner are bound to be included. Of the latter exponents, James Redfield and Neale Donald Walsch have gained a certain reputation among those who wish for a renaissance of belief. One thinks of Diana Cooper and "the Ascended Masters," Louise Hay, Kryon, and the Indigo Children. Cultural elements such as "channeling" might be regarded as merely spiritualist mediumship under another name, but this highlights the difficulty of pinning down any definable direction for the New Age, which is mainly due to the eclecticism of its followers. A wide range of the means of expression is seen as a virtue, as is a tolerance of diversity. It is this aspect that perhaps separates the New Age movement from the aims of those in the 1960s. Then, the overwhelming desire was to "liberate" areas of society and culture that were seen as repressive or archaic. The steady toppling of shibboleths was the most important aim, one which would have the result, it was believed, of creating a truly liberal society. Attitudes to sex, drugs, politics, race, and equality *did* become more relaxed—until attitudes that had once seemed revolutionary had been absorbed into the mainstream. The noticeable effect was to dull the original spirit, never so evident as what happened to rock music. Once the soundtrack of youthful rebellion, it steadily became flatulent and empty and never recovered.[226]

One of the true minority preoccupations in the 1960s and 1970s was the occult. Magick, including the Tarot and the Kabbalah, was still regarded as something sinister. This worked to the advantage of those who were involved with the discipline as they were left alone to their research. What the New Age did when it arrived in the mid-1980s was to embrace every belief, creed, and ritual that could be found, even inventing a few new ones on the way.

> *"New Age is not a world religion but a modern form of spiritual mysticism. It is an effort to follow one's own spiritual path and express the essential divinity that is present in all living things. The realization of this 'holy oneness' is left for each person to interpret and implement for themselves."*[228]

The original dwellers in Hippiedom were never very sure of their relationship with "God." Unwilling to be associated with any creed that could be seen as patriarchal or puritanical (which undoubtedly twentieth-century Christianity was) they were loath to make any alliance with "the universe." Embracing Eastern religion was never going to be the answer, but it does appear that the New Age in its espousing of "spirit" or the universal force has improved on the need for a belief system that reflects Aquarian values. Identifying New Age ideas, which truly do subscribe to this criterion, would seem essential in order to assess the validity of the movement.

The "interconnectedness of everything," a holographic approach to the universe, would seem to be a cornerstone of belief amongst New Agers. An astral plane which contains angels, ascended masters, guides, and guardians is thought to exist alongside an earthly one. This "universal mind" is seen as greater than any physical reality, and universal love a panacea for all ills. Death is not an end, merely life in a different form. Divine guidance is seen as having more to offer than scepticism or rationalism, although the hope is that eventually science and spirituality will be in harmony. Relationships with others are important as they affect personal karma. The sacred nature of people and places is emphasized in New Age doctrine as evidence of the healing nature of creation. All of these principles seem perfectly sound, if not particularly original. It is the assumption that a particular approach is always a given that has evoked criticisms of the New Age philosophy.

Adherents of traditional disciplines are wary of New Agers who seek to espouse those disciplines without study and application, regarding anyone who does not adopt that approach as superficial. Vagueness, trivialising, and lack of understanding are all present in the New Age, though perhaps all schools of thought that are primarily mystical are always vulnerable to such criticism. The emphasis on individual vision rather negates an empirical approach, so the absence of any scholarship (often evident in New Age writings on the internet) naturally leads to impatience from those who have spent their lives in research.[229]

Rational thinkers are sceptical of everything about the New Age. Ayn Rand denied that a thing was worth knowing if it could not be known through analysis and used the word "mysticism" to denounce those who are hostile to reason. Neal Donner denies this but still maintains that *"...we must also part company with those...carefree romantics who suggest that discipline or careful study inevitably stifles the spirit."*[230]

Today's instant access to information is a two-edged sword, as the medium can so easily become the message as McLuhan predicted. Accusations of being anti-intellectual and dismissive of established thought are often levelled at proponents of New Age beliefs and these attacks do seem justified. It will be interesting to see if the New Age will be able to sustain its influence or whether another more radical movement will overtake it.

Arise, Arthur...

Ecological issues, which certainly came to the fore in the 1960s, were to become in the 1990s a *cause célèbre*. One of the most notorious and celebrated figures who dramatically appeared at this time was *King Arthur Pendragon*. His biographer suggests:

> *"If you picture him then, then, as a Dark Ages battle chieftain, a soldier, trained in the Roman army, leading a wild band of Nomadic horsemen in defense of Britain against the Barbarian invasion; if you picture him fighting, berserker style, on horseback, charging into the fray, sword flailing and flashing red in the sun; a leader not a follower, laughing in the face of death; if you imagine him carousing after battle...then you have some picture of our own Arthur."* [231]

A figure, whose role in many ways echoes the original warrior king, could with only a modicum of imagination be seen as the perfect cornerstone for a definition of the New Age. The only problem with that thesis is that Arthur himself would not wish to be seen as being associated with the New Age in any shape or form. But, for the purposes of our study, King Arthur Pendragon being an activist, a defender of his kingdom (as he would think of it), and leader of his "warband" is an appropriate icon. [232] Ashe, writing of the original King Arthur, concludes, *"His life is a curious mixture of grace and squalor..."* [233] A description of this Arthur could not be bettered! Headstrong, indulgent, sometimes foolish, but the perfect foil for the insensitive, greedy, materialistic powers who would destroy England as soon as look at it. The Prescotts and Tescos of this world, insensitive, stupid, tyrants whose cupidity demands to be defied by a wild, bearded man with courage and conviction. Timothy Rothwell, once a Hells Angel, decided in 1987 that he was the reincarnation of England's archetypal hero, acquired an Excalibur, and changed his name by deed poll. [234] It would be unwise and unfair to regard Arthur Pendragon as anyone but a positive force for good.

The New Age might have emerged in the 1980s as a response to what was seen then as a repressive and materialistic government. [235] Road building schemes (at Twyford Down and Newbury, among others) were seen as unnecessary and a vicious destruction of the countryside. As C.J. Stone, the biographer of Arthur Pendragon notes, *"The road protests can be seen as the revolt of the Earth ...the revolt of Nature against the tyranny of the roads."*[236] Certainly, the images of road protesters shown on national television were dominated by the figure in cloak and circlet striding among the:

"Wild. Unmanageable. Free. With tattered clothing and body piercings, with tattoos and dreadlocks, with feathers and bells, playing penny whistles and cantering drums, they seemed like something out of story books or legend, like nothing less than the fairy folk of long ago." [237]

Besides attempting to halt construction on the site, to prevent the felling of trees became the prime objective of the protesters. The tree became a symbol of everything that Arthur's warband stood for. As C.J. Stone puts it:

"And what is a tree? It is a life form, a living being. Older than a man, rugged and deep-rooted, clutching the earth with a fierce grip, a tree stands for all that is solitary and unwavering in the soul of man, for all that is ancient and connected."[238]

Arthur Pendragon likes to be known as a "druid activist." Rollo Maughfling, head of the Glastonbury Order of Druids, was instrumental in Arthur becoming a druid. He invited him to take part in a Beltane ceremony at the top of Glastonbury Tor. At the end of the proceedings, Rollo signalled for Arthur to produce Excalibur.

"At that moment the sun came out from behind a cloud and a shaft of sunlight hit the sword like a grand of fire. The sword shattered the sunlight sending prismatic sprays of dazzling colour into the air. It was an explosion of light."[239]

In an otherwise sceptical book review, David Martin quite neatly summarises the uniting of Paganism and radicalism in the common cause of protest.

"So the original bedrock of shamanistic ecstasy has again been exposed to view, and neo-Paganism in an eco-mystical mode stands poised

to challenge our exploitative and consumerist capitalist society. Neo-Pagans of the world unite! The oldest and most 'natural' layer of religion is once more adaptive for a world where nature has been raped and the environment polluted."[240]

The fight was hard and for Arthur—arrest, prison, and court proceedings were his rewards. But this in no way stopped him for an instant. As Clausewitz tells us in his masterly work *The Art of War*:

"Kindhearted people might of course think there was some ingenious way to disarm or defeat an enemy without too much bloodshed, and might imagine this is the true goal of the art of war. Pleasant as it sounds, it is a fallacy that must be exposed: war is such a dangerous business that the mistakes which come from kindness are the very worst. The maximum use of force is in no way incompatible with the simultaneous use of the intellect."

And who were these protesters? Who were the self-styled denizens of the New Age?

"They came from all backgrounds, from all classes: from the public school educated upper-middle class, from the professional middle class, from the aristocracy, from the working class and the underclass, from the drop-out class, the traveller and biker communities."[241]

Let them all come, let them discover the great gain from being at one with the land. Celebrating, loving, living, and above all—being together in harmony. The planet needs consideration, respect, and above all, commitment. This is the time; the time is ours. As for Arthur, ancient and modern, *"One day we may discover that the Fact has been more truly potent than the Legend, and that King Arthur has returned, after all, by abdication."[242]*

Glastonbury—The Circle Complete

Geoffrey Ashe, writing in 1968, did not know how prophetic his words would be:

> *"Enthusiasts have predicted that Glastonbury's future, in some way which cannot yet be foreseen, will be greater than its past...many who have taken part in Glastonbury's renewal find themselves exploring the mystery by other paths."[243]*

Half a century before, Dion Fortune had moved to Glastonbury to establish a community on the land now occupied by the Chalice Well gardens.[244] She believed that neither the Pagan nor the Christian ethos had the monopoly regarding Avalon.

> *"...the enigmatic quality of some of the monuments, and the intangible nature of its medieval and modern traditions, represent the greatest gifts which it makes to modern religion."*

Dion Fortune, well aware of the topography, Archangel Michael is the bringer of light. The guide to the underworld. The world inside the Tor.

She did believe that Glastonbury was the "gateway to the unseen" and the Tor was the place where all four elements, Fire, Air, Earth and Water met. As Frederick Bligh Bond wrote:

> *"Then ye grasse shal bee as glasse*
> *And ye schal see ye mysterie*
> *Deep downe hit lyes from pryinge eies*
> *And safelie slepes, while vigil kepes*
> *Ye Company.*
> *(How doe) ye dry bonys stir and shake*
> *And eche to eche hys fellowe seekes*
> *Soone comes agayne what once hath bene*
> *And Glastonys glory shal be scene."[245]*

In the early 1960s, Glastonbury was to most a very sleepy market town. The annual cricket festival was perhaps the most exciting event of the year. By the end of that decade, with the advent of the change of consciousness that we have already discussed, came a change. *"The years around 1970 were...the Second Romantic Movement. One aspect of this was a profound desire to reinvest the world with magick and mystery..."* as Ronald Hutton succinctly puts it, and goes on to tell us, *"Glastonbury began to fill up with young dreamers in jeans, kaftans, and Afghan coats..."*[246] This writer can certainly vouch for the accuracy of that remark, as he was one of them!

Probably the advent of the first Glastonbury Rock Festival in 1971 was the turning point.[247] Alternative types were certainly not welcome at that time in its recent history, yet as we know in the twenty-first century, that has all changed.

> *"The visitor wanders through the shops lining the two main streets and the courtyards and alleyways beyond them, brushing against Indian shawls and Peruvian silver jewelry, and locally made images of Green Men and pregnant goddesses, hearing the cool voices of women sing from compact discs about queens and wizards and earth magic, passing stands of cards decorated with native Americana, animal spirits, witches and zodiacs, and browsing through bookshelves in which characters from early Celtic literature rub shoulders with shamans, dowsers and The Goddess."*[248]

Glastonbury is now many things to many people. With a population of several thousand, it is sometimes difficult not to think that everyone there is some sort of psychic practitioner. To a great many ordinary Somerset folks, it is just where their families have lived for centuries. Perhaps the place was always lying dormant, ready for the massive interest it would attract, and the power of the place never actually went away—it couldn't.

> *"In the old times, the myth centred on place: on specific places. The myth made up stories about those places. The places drew people to them. The people were entranced by those places. They gathered.*

They told each other stories. They span webs of enchantment to explain themselves to each other. It was the places that told the stories. They were the enchanted places, the holy places. The people were made holy by them."[249]

The Glastonbury Zodiac, that extraordinary topographical phenomenon that extends over the moors is almost inevitable proof, if any more were needed, of the sacred nature of Glastonbury and its environs. In 1574, John Dee plotted a map of the area demonstrating the presence of heavenly constellations on the ground. *"The stares which agree with their reproductions on the ground do lye onlie on the celestial path of the Sonne, moon and planets..."* It was Kathryn Maltwood, publishing anonymously in 1935 *A Guide to Glastonbury's Temple of the Stars,* which drew the most attention to these representational figures, each one illustrating not only the astrological signs, but the significant stages of the Arthurian Quest and even the location of the Holy Grail.[250] Maltwood's belief that the features were engineered by Sumerian priests falls into the realm of those other "visitors from afar" theories that abound with regard to Glastonbury, though none the less possible for all that.

Glastonbury has in recent years played host to the "Cult of the Goddess."

"She is the goddess of the dead Lady of the West. Love, music, beauty, dance, fertility, and childbirth are hers. '...those who believed that prehistoric society had been matriarchal, and its religion centred upon a Great Goddess, both being destroyed by warlike and patriarchal brutes who had laid the foundation of all the ills of modern society."[251]

In the American state of Arizona, the town of Sedona has become the New Age centre of that part of the country. The Arthurian story has become part of an international language, but in America, the support for the Arthurian "tradition" has been from American scholars and ordinary citizens. As Ronald Hutton remarks, *"... whether or not the New Jerusalem is easier to find in the New World than the Old, it is certainly easier to market there."*[252] Any scepticism has risen from the ranks of British scholars. With the coming of the New Age, it is perhaps the first time for centuries that succeeding generations have been sympathetic through a common belief.[253] The seed of spirituality that was sown in the 60s has grown and blossomed in the twenty-first century and it is marvellous to behold. The current interest in the Grail is no random occurrence; it is perhaps the acknowledgment of a deep desire to find meaning in an existence that was threatened so acutely with the rise of industrialisation. This is the test of the Aquarian Age to discover a balance between technology and faith. Materialism is the manifestation of the darker side of man's nature. Darkness fears light and so the emphasis upon consumerism as a way of life. Never before has the tyranny of cultural and economic domination been so evident.

Yet the key to understanding lies within us. We are poised at the beginning of the Quest, and this journey is as significant as Avalon was to the questing knights. In our landscape, wood, lake, cavern; all contain mystery. After the Hallows have been returned in the Faery Autumn peace will return. We must not stray from that path until we see Arthur in all his glory. As William G. Gray unequivocally reminds us, *"Man will never amount to anything until he knows who he is."*[254]

ENDNOTES

1. Stephen Coote, *John Keats—A Life* (London: Hodder and Stoughton, 1995) p.84.
2. Wolfram von Eschenbach, *Parsifal* (London: Penguin, 1980) p.240.
3. Isabel Cooper-Oakley, *Masonry and Medieval Mysticism*. (London: Theosophical Publishing House, 1900) p.149.
4. Such woodworking devices certainly existed at the time.
5. Michael Baigent, Richard Leigh, and Henry Lincoln, *The Holy Blood and The Holy Grail* (London: Corgi 1982).
6. Valentin Tomberg, *Meditations on the Tarot—A Journey into Christian Hermeticism*, (New York: Putnam 2003) p.60.
7. Tomberg, p.67.
8. Teilhard de Chardin, *Future of Man* (London: Fontana, 1968) p.89.
9. Ibid.
10. Avicenna, *Alchemical Studies* (Basel:1593).
11. Marie-Louise von Franz, *C.G. Jung, His Myths in Our Time*. (Toronto: Inner City Books, 1988).
12. It has never been satisfactorily resolved as to what the answer to the Grail Question might have been. Gareth Knight suggests "that which is excluded from the Trinity"—meaning "the female." Thus, the Grail as a symbol of the Goddess is confirmed.
13. One part of him is missing—his member—consumed by fishes. Isis fashions a new one from the clay of the Nile. It must have been a successful addition, as Horus was later conceived by Isis and Osiris.
14. Michio Kaku, *Parallel Worlds—The Science of Alternative Universes and Our Future in the Cosmos* (London: Penguin, 2005) p.243.
15. Papus, *The Tarot of the Bohemians* (San Francisco: Melvin Powers Wilshire Book Company) p.205.
16. Heraclitus, *Fragment* (New York: Penguin, 2003) p.102.
17. Dion Fortune, *Sane Occultism* (Loughborough: Aquarian Press, 1987) p. 284.
18. E. Harding, *Women's Mysteries* (New York: Rider, 1971) p.17.
19. Hans Leisegang, *Die Gnosis* (Leipzig: 1924) p.51.
20. Campbell, p.382.
21. T.S. Eliot, *Collected Poems 1909-1962* (London: Faber and Faber, 1963) p.63.

22. *The Vulgate Cycle—Queste del Saint Graal* (London: Penguin Classics, 2004) p.56.

23. Sir Thomas Malory, *The Death of King Arthur* (London: Penguin, 1995) p.197.

24. Lewis Carroll, *Lewis Carroll's Diaries Volume 2 January to December 1856* (London: Lewis Carroll Society, 1994) p.67.

25. Kaku, p.301

26. Carlos Castaneda, *Journey to Ixtlan* (London: The Bodley Head, 1972) p.252.

27. Robert E.L. *Masters and Jean Houston, Psychedelic Art* (New York: Grove Press, 1968) p.17.

28. Ibid p.89.

29. Ibid p.19.

30. Timothy Leary, New York Times, Sept. 20, 1966.

31. Musicians, such as the Beatles and Jimi Hendrix, were in the vanguard as well as many writers, poets, and artists. The writer was there too!

32. Masters, p.96.

33. Gardner, p.150.

34. Jay Stevens, *Storming Heaven* (New York: Grove Press, 1987) p.257.

35. David Hume, On Human Nature and Understanding (London: Collier, 1962) p.230.

36. David Deutsch, *The Fabric of Reality* (London: Penguin, 1998) p.145.

37. Brian Greene, *The Fabric of the Cosmos: Space, Time, and the Texture of Reality.* (New York: Kopf, 2004) p.74.

38. Fred Alan Wolf, *Parallel Universes* (New York: Simon and Schuster, 1988) p.56.

39. Michio Kaku, *Parallel Worlds* (London: Penguin, 2005) p.149.

40. Term coined by Gottfried Leibniz in 1710, an attempt to account for the presence of evil in a world created by an omnipotent God. Theodicy concludes that God's world is just, as it is, the "best of all possible worlds."

41. Campbell, p.269.

42. Wolf, p.78.

43. Virginia Woolf, *Hyde Park Gate News* (Modern Fiction) (London: Hesperus Books, 2006) p.68.

44. Daniel Dennet, *Consciousness Explained* (London: Little Brown, 1991) p.218.

45. Tomberg p.67.

46. Ibid p.68.

47. Ken Carey, *Starseed: The Third Millennium—Living in the Posthistoric World* (San Francisco: Harper, 1991) p.127.

48. R.D. Nelson and others, *Correlations of Continuous Random Data with Major World Events* (Princeton University, 2002).

49. Sir James Jeans, *The Mysterious Universe* (Cambridge: The University Press, 1932) p.186.

50. There is apparently the "Old Mysterianism." Leibniz and Samuel Johnson were advocates of its principles.

51. Donald Zagier and others, *The 1-2-3 of Modular Forms* (Berlin: Springer-Verlag, 2008) p.70.

52. Lewis Carroll, *The Annotated Alice (Definitive Edition)*—ed. Martin Gardner (London: Penguin, 2001) p. xxiii.

53. Alfred Jarry, *Gestes et Opinions du Docteur Faustroll Pataphysicien* (Austin, Texas: Exact Change, 1996) II, viii.

54. Jarry II, ix.

55. Max Planck, *Eight Lectures on Theoretical Physics* (London: Dover Publications, 1997) p.56.

56. It is only fair to declare my own affiliations with Somerset. I was born nine miles from the isle of Avalon and Glastonbury Tor was within sight of my parents' home.

57. Marion Zimmer Bradley in her Mists of Avalon depicts this hidden, otherworldly quality extremely well.

58. Lucius Apuleius, *The Golden Ass,* Trans. P.G. Walsh (Oxford: Oxford World's Classics, 1997) p.189.

59. Campbell, p.199 (footnote).

60. Otto Rhan, *Crusade Against the Grail* (Rochester, Vermont: Inner Traditions, 2006) p. 201.

61. Rahn, p.176.

62. Nigel Graddon, *Otto Rahn and the Quest for the Holy Grail: The Amazing Life of the Real Indiana Jones* (San Francisco, USA: Adventures Unlimited Press, 2008) p.89.

63. Campbell, p.376.

64. Henry Adams Bellows (trans.) *The Poetic Edda: The Mythological Poems* (St. Paul, Minn. USA: Dover Publications, 2004) p.178.

65. Campbell, p.390.

66. John 3, viii.

67. Sean O'Brien, "Straight to Screen," Times Literary Supplement, August 6th 2010 (p.19).

68. Terry Gilliam, Salman Rushdie Talks with Terry Gilliam.

69. William James, *The Varieties of Religious Experience* (London: Collier-MacMillan, 1961) p.304.

70. John Michell, *Confessions of a Radical Traditionalist* (Vermont: Dominion, 2005) p.252.

71. Laplace, *Essai philosophique Sur les Probabilities* tr. F. Wilson Truscott, F. Lincoln Emory (New York: Dover Publications, 1951) Introduction.

72. Arthur Schopenhauer, *The World as Will and Representation Vol I* (St. Paul Minnesota: Dover Publications, 1965) p.79.

73. Tomberg, p.89.

74. The title of a TV series starring Oliver Tobias and made in 1972 at Publow in Somerset. The writer was an extra in several episodes, playing the part of a Celtic warrior.

75. John Morris *The Age of Arthur: A History of the British Isles from 350 to 650* (London: Weidenfeld and Nicholson, 1973) p.70.

76. Geoffrey Ashe *The Quest for Arthur's Britain* (London Granada Publishing, 1968) p.183.

77. Writing in 1940 of Belgian refugees, William G. Gray's account spans the years, "...the women are the ones who suffer the most in war. Loved men who die in battle can never be given back to them, nor will the gap in their lives ever be filled...this awful misery and anxiety... they try not to show it, and their bravery is greater than anything..." Alan Richardson. The Old Sod—The Odd Life and Inner Work of William G. Gray (London: Ignotus: 2003) p.107.

78. Ashe p.47.

79. p.60.

80. We only abuse them in later years, Wellington or Churchill, for instance.

81. Morris p.506.

82. p. 507, 508.

83. Ashe p.56.

84. Ashe p.115.

85. Nicholas R. Mann, *Energy Secrets of Glastonbury Tor* (Glastonbury: Green Magic, 2004), p.92.

86. Quoted in Ronald Hutton *Witches, Druids and King Arthur* (London: Hambledon, 2003), p.48.

87. Hutton p.78.

88. p.49.

89. John Grigsby, *Warriors of the Wasteland* (London: Watkins Publishing, 2002) p. xix.

90. James P. Carley, *Glastonbury Abbey: The Holy House at the head of the Moors Adventurous* (Glastonbury: Gothic Image, 2006).

91. T.F. Dexter, *Cornwall—The Land of the Gods* (London: Watts & Co., 1932), p.26.

92. Alan Richardson, *Priestess—The life and Magic of Dion Fortune* (Wellingborough: Aquarian Press, 1987).

93. Robert Graves, *The White Goddess* (London: Faber and Faber, 1961), p.109.

94. Geoffrey Ashe, *Camelot and the Vision of Avalon* (London: William Heinemann, 1972), p.27.

95. John Michell, *The New View over Atlantis* (London: Thames and Hudson, 1983) p.20.

96. Frederick Bligh Bond, *The Gate of Remembrance* (Wellingborough: Thorsons, 1918) p.104.

97. Viktor Shauberger, "The Water Wizard" had this to say: "In every drop of water dwells the Godhead...there also dwells life, the Soul of the 'First' substance...more energy is encapsulated in every drop of good spring water than an average-sized PowerStation is presently able to produce."

98. Richardson p.78.

99. Ashe p.151.

100. Michell p.183.

101. Morris p.87.

102. Ashe p.160.

103. p.4

104. William G. Gray suggests that "Each race carries its own unique record of superphysical and subjective phenomena through its bloodstream, and these memories constitute our fables, legends, gods, heroes..." Richardson p. 225, 226.

105. Graves tells us that Arthur was one of the "...Three Crimson-stained Ones of Britain...to be (thus) is to be a sacred king..." The White Goddess p.324.

106. Ashe p.232.

107. It is Geoffrey of Monmouth who casts him as the spiritual guide to Arthur and who also gives him the name Merlinus rather than Merdinus, which is too close to being, in French at least, a questionable pun.

108. Richard Cavendish, *King Arthur & The Grail–The Arthurian Legends and their Meaning* (London: Weidenfeld and Nicholson, 1978) p.110.

109. Grigsby p.50.

110. The art of the swordsmith was shrouded in secrecy, legend, and magick. Wayland's Smithy (near the White Horse at Uffington) may have originally been a labyrinth, as is Glastonbury Tor.

111. Ashe p.102.

112. W.E. Butler, *The Magician: His training and work* (London: Aquarian Press) p.195.

113. Following his Celtic forbears, he would probably have preferred the latter. Celt means "to fight" and there is no evidence Arthur was greatly attached to Roman ways.

114. Derived from Caladfwlch or Calad-bolg, meaning "hard lightning." Jove is depicted with three thunderbolts: chance, destiny, and providence. The eagle, sacred to Jove, is associated with fire like Vulcan at his forge. Excalibur is said to have originally been borne by the Irish hero Cu Chulainn. Geoffrey of Monmouth introduces the sword Caliburn or Chalybs (steel) into his narrative and depicts it as a gift from Avalon, or more precisely the mists of Avalon, which create the Lake of Wonder.

115. The Lady of the Lake protects Arthur and Lancelot, but in a cruel irony, Merlin will fall in love with her and the reward for his desire will be imprisonment in the Perilous Forest, thus forever depriving Arthur of his magickal helper.

116. The tradition of making offerings to the river god Silvanus may have prompted the ritual of casting Excalibur into the Lake.

117. Cavendish p.55.

118. William G. Gray, *The Outlook on our Western Way* (New York Samuel Weiser, 1980) p.2.

119. Interesting speculations as to assigning twelve to thirteen arise!

120. With the Fool (0) standing outside the circle and making thirteen.

121. It is telling that the giants whom knights are constantly called to fight represent "brute force and ignorance, mindless irresponsibility, and the destructiveness of greed and lust" (Cavendish p. 80). There is

more than a hint that the hero is fait accompli an aristocrat, the giant always a commoner.

122. This goddess is associated with witchcraft, being often accompanied by hares—often the witches' familiar.

123. In Mithraism, associated with the Sun and also indicating the first grade of initiate.

124. *The Mabinogion,* trans. Jeffrey Gautz (London: Penguin, 1976) p.189.

125. "Arthur, in taking on the traits of various other immortal kings, acquired the Welsh king's goat" (Ashe Note p.7), suggesting that the king was born under the sign of Capricorn. Indications of his birthdate in Geoffrey of Monmouth are compatible with this view.

126. The followers of Attis sacrificed rams to their god.

127. "All that remains of the 1360 church, itself the second on the site— its predecessor fell in an earthquake on the inauspicious date of 11th September 1275." Grigsby p. xxiii.

128. Grigsby p.38.

129. The writer's grandfather Rev. E.A.H. Strong was the rector of St. Bridget's church at Breane. His grandson also married a Frances Bridget Sarler.

130. "...said to derive from the Irish Bec-eru meaning 'Little Ireland.'" Ashe p.86.

131. She is the Swan Maiden, escaping the attentions of men by flying into the heavens.

132. Jones includes every female figure in the Arthurian canon, which is too much of a scattergun approach.

133. Kathy Jones, *In the Nature of Avalon—Goddess Pilgrimages in Glastonbury's Sacred Landscape* (Ariadne Publications).

134. "...goddess of smithcraft, the alchemical art in which metallic ores are heated in the fire until the impurities slough off, leaving pure metals, like gold and silver which are transformed into articles of great beauty." Jones.

135. Hutton p.53.

136. Again, the number of guardians of the Grail varies in this tradition.

137. "The Sumerians believed that scorpions...were guardians of the gateway of the Sun." D.J. Conway, Animal Magick (Minnesota: Llewellyn, 1996) p. 207. Mithraism too "symbolised life and death, the rising and setting Sun," by respectively a Bull and a Scorpion. Mithraism is a soldiers' religion.

138. Grigsby p.134.
139. Alan Richardson, Unpublished Essay "The Depths of the Lake," 1989. The writer was most gratified to receive this from A.R.
140. William G. Gray describes the unfortunate prelate him as "...a 'Dark Twin,' a holy surrogate who was ritually slain to enable the King [Henry II] to continue for another fixed period." Richardson p.104.
141. Guinevere may also have an association with the boar—Orc Triath.
142. *The Anglo-Saxon World—An Anthology* (Oxford O.U.P., 1982), p.57.
143. Richardon–Essay.
144. Cavendish p.44.
145. Ibid. p.52.
146. The Grail may have been guarded by a different number of maidens. It is possible that they totalled nine. "The breath of nine maidens keeps it boiling" is a reference to Annwn's Cauldron in a poem by Taliesin (Grigsby p.194). Graves suggests these may be a manifestation of the nine daughters of Zeus.
147. W.B. Yeats, *The Celtic Twilight—Myth, Fantasy and Folklore* (Dorset: Prism Press Dorset, 1999) p.100, 101.
148.
149. Fred Gettings, *Dictionary of Astrology* (London: Rourtledge & Kegan Paul, 1985) p.105.
150. Carlos Castaneda, *Journey to Ixtlan* (London: Bodley Head, 1972) p.54.
151. Hutton p.77.
152. p.61.
153. Dion Fortune described the feeling of "...(standing) in the great nave, looking towards the high altar, is like standing waist-deep in a swift mountain stream." Knight (Seminar).
154. Dion Fortune was The Priestess. She saw herself, and with good reason, as not only Isis but also Hathor, the consort of Horus the King.
155. The Tor is dedicated to the elements of Fire and Air, Chalice Hill to Water, and Wearyall Hill to Earth.
156. p.64.
157. Bligh Bond p.45.
158. Hutton p.60.
159. Dion Fortune, *Avalon of the Heart* (Wellingborough: Aquarian Press, 1978) p.72.

160. Israel Regardie, *The Middle Pillar* (Minnesota: Llewellyn, 1970) p.136.

161. Fortune p.2.

162. p.29.

163. Nicholas R. Mann, *Energy Secrets of Glastonbury Tor* (Glastonbury: Green Magic, 2004).

164. Alan Richardson, *Magical Gateways* (Minnesota: Llewellyn Publications, 1992) p.107.

165. Ashe p.26.

166. Carlos Castenada, *Tales of Power* (London: Penguin, 1974) p.237.

167. Gray p.42.

168. "It is here that a very curious point of contact is reached between East and West. The Early Vegetation Rites recorded in the Indian Rig Veda hymns stress the 'Freeing of the Waters.'"

169. "Thou Indra has slain Vitra by thy Vigour, thou hast set free the rivers." *Chalice Well—A Short History* (Chalice Well Trust, 1975) p.14.

170. *The Diaries of Franz Kafka*, edited by Max Brod (London: Penguin, 1972) p.417.

171. As assistant editor of *The Egoist*, Eliot proofread Ulysses before it was published as a serial in that literary magazine. Eliot was at that time a champion of Joyce.

172. *Selected Prose of T.S. Eliot* (London: Faber and Faber, 1975) p.175.

173. Written prophetically in 1939.

174. p.290.

175. Eliot's similarity to the writer Thomas Pynchon, also an American, might be commented upon. In an introduction to an early novel *Slow Learner*, Pynchon remarks, "Somewhere I had come up with the notion that one's personal life had nothing to do with fiction, when the truth, as everyone knows is nearly the direct opposite."

176. *The Waste Land—A Collection of Critical Essays* (London: Macmillan and Co Ltd.,1968) p.40.

177. p.196.

178. p.222.

179. In *Poetry and Drama* (1951), Eliot put forward his own "impersonal theory of poetry," suggesting that "The poet's mind is in fact a receptacle for seizing and storing up numberless feelings, phrases, images, which remain there until all the particles which can unite to form a new compound are present together."

180. Peter Ackroyd, *T.S. Eliot* (London: Hamish Hamilton, 1984) p.110.
181. *Critical Essays* p.26.
182. p.39.
183. Ackroyd p. 104.
184. p.107.
185. Eliot lived in an era when the printed word was the paramount medium and public lecture were still popular.
186. Ackroyd p.213.
187. Although "East Coker" is one of the Four Quartets, no satisfactory explanation has ever been put forward as to why Eliot should wish his ashes to lie in such an obscure Somerset village. Perhaps he was following the dictum of Thomas à Kempis: "Strive to be unknown, and to be thought of no account."
188. The plaque on the wall in East Coker church commemorating Eliot is small and fitted slightly askew—at least it was in 1969 when the writer made a pilgrimage there, sleeping in a field nearby and waking to a pale December dawn.
189. Gray p.55.
190. Grigsby p.125.
191. Cuchulainn harrows hell and returns with his prize.
192. Gwyn ap Nudd (Light, son of Darkness) is king of the fairy folk and lord of Annwn. His symbol is the Night Eagle, i.e., the owl. Samhain was his time and "accompanied by immortal companions on horseback and a whole pack of huge white hounds with glowing red eyes," he collects souls. Glastonbury Tor was mainly where he did this, Tor not only stands for a high hill but also means door or gateway. Gwyn also is to be found anywhere that Earth and Sky meet. Gray (p.18).
193. Or Kerridwen, a Moon goddess linked to Kerid. a Cornish deity active at the autumn equinox.
194. Grigsby p.185.
195. p.187.
196. John Heath-Stubbs, *Charles Williams* (London: Longmans, Green & Co., 1955) p.29.
197. A title seemingly possessed by those initiates who had tasted immortality from the cauldron and were reborn as the salmon itself (Grigsby p.183).

198. Who it is said hid the Grail in Chalice Hill at the foot of Glastonbury Tor.

199. Grantz p.18.

200. Grigsby p.62.

201. p.55.

202. The Waste Land, being as it is, may be punishment for the crime of rape and murder of the Grail maidens.

203. Yeats depicts the whole enterprise as ridiculous. "A fool with a shining vessel." p.100.

204. *The Mabinogion* p.248, 249.

205. Eliot, *Critical Essays* p. 110.

206. Dan Brown in his spurious *The DaVinci Code* being the greatest culprit.

207. Cavendish p.181.

208. Heath Stubbs p.36.

209. Knight asks, "But what of the other hallows of the Graal, the spear the cup, the stone, or the cruets of white and red? Great mystery surrounds their origin as well as their fate. If we read the earliest Graal stories, we find there is much to suggest that the Graal itself had a faery origin. Was the rich Fisher King in his boat upon the waters, who directed Percival to the mysterious castle that was at first invisible to the eye one of the Faery kind? In later legend the Graal winners took a strange boat, called the Ship of Solomon, in which they took the Graal to Sarras, which seems an inner aspect of the Holy Land, just as Logres is an inner level of Albion. What was the mission of Joseph of Arimathea in all of this? Is the belief that he was bringing back the Graal to Avalon, a realisation that the hallows were about to be returned to their faery origins?" (Seminar).

210. Richardson p.131.

211. p.110

212. Gray p.2

213. Israel Regardie, *The Middle Pillar* (Minnesota: Llewellyn, 1970) p. 39.

214. As Dion Fortune said, "it is the land and its ways that make history, far more than the will of kings." (Gareth Knight—Dion Fortune Seminar, 2 September 2006.)

215. Knight.

216. Known also as St. Bride's Mount or Beckery (from the Irish beag Eiru or perhaps bheach na haorai—mound of the bees). It is also known as Beckery Ridge (or the Salmon Ridge or the Salmon of the West, from its unusual shape). It is located at the foot of Wearyall Hill and originally established about a sacred (Bride's) well.

217. Knight.

218. The writer is grateful to the Webmaster of Bridesmound for this insight.

219. Knight.

220. Carlos Castaneda, *Tales of Power* (London: Hodder & Stoughton, 1975) p.282.

221. For the complete etymology of the word Grail, the reader should consult the copious amounts of Sangreal literature.

222. Richardson p.217.

223. Yeats p.101.

224. Gray p.30.

225. Derek Taylor, *It Was Twenty Years Ago Today* (London: Transworld, 1987) p.167.

226. Taylor p. 189.

227. p.232.

228. It can now be seen that the advent and rapid demise of punk in 1977 was most certainly a false dawn.

229. In the twenty-first century, some are mainstream authors.

230. Unknown Source.

231. Dr. Ad Putter, a respected medievalist, told the writer recently of his surprise upon discovering his books filed under "mystical" in a bookshop.

232. Neal Donner, *Mysticism and the Idea of Freedom*, 1997.

233. C.J. Stone, *The Trials of Arthur—The life and Times of a Modern-Day King* (London: Element, 2003) p.50.

234. And the writer who has had the honour of meeting him certainly has no wish to offend Arthur.

235. Ashe, QAB p.95.

236. "He is clearly a sincere natural mystic, whose very strong libertarian political convictions are bound up with a sense of guidance by supernatural forces. His belief in reincarnation was stimulated by the experience of vivid dreams and reveries, known since childhood, which seemed to him to be memories of previous lifetimes. His

assumption of the identity of King Arthur in 1987 was precipitated by a series of apparent signs and omens." This is the CJS 238 Appendix 3 witness statement prepared by Prof. Ronald E Hutton for the trial of Arthur Pendragon at Southwark Crown Court, in November 1997, regarding Arthur's right to carry the sword Excalibur. (Stone p. 238).

237. One might argue that the policies of our own Prime Minister in 2006, Tony Blair, were a far greater threat to national liberty.

238. C.J. Stone, *The Trials of Arthur—The life and Times of a Modern-Day King* (London: Element, 2003) p.131.

239. Stone p.130.

240. p.155.

241. p.77.

242. David Martin in a review of Brian Hayden, *Shamans, Sorcerers and Saints. A Prehistory of Religion.* (Smithsonian Washington, 2006), Time Literary Supplement 24 Mar. 2006.

243. p.130.

244. Ashe, Camelot p.19.

245. Ashe p. 125.

246. Dion Fortune's grave is in Glastonbury Cemetery and not that easy to discover. Persevere!

247. Frederick Bligh Bond, *The Gate of Remembrance* (Wellingborough: Thorsons, 1918).

248. Hutton p.50.

249. In 1971, Michael Eavis was at pains to describe the event as "an earth fayre." This description of the event did not stop my band playing there in that year. It was free, you got a communal tent to sleep in, and you got fed. Not bad, eh? I've never been since—not through any personal pique, I would hasten to add.

250. Hutton p.59.

251. Stone p.79.

252. Just outside the medieval village of Butleigh.

253. Hutton p.53.

254. p.54.

255. And a great affinity between the generations with music. Jimi Hendrix is as popular now as he was when he first appeared in England in 1966.

256. Richardson p.227.

BIBLIOGRAPHY

Apuleius, Lucius. *The Golden Ass.* Trans. P.G. Walsh. Oxford: Oxford World's Classics.

Ackroyd, Peter, and T.S. Eliot. London: Hamish Hamilton, 1984.

Ashe, Geoffrey. *King Arthur's Avalon—The Story of Glastonbury.* London: Collins, 1957.
— *The Quest for Arthur's Britain.* London: Grandala Publishing, 1968
— *Camelot and the Vision of Avalon.* London: William Heinemann, 1972.
— *Mythology of the British Isles.* London: Methuen, 1990.

Avicenna. *Alchemical Studies.* Basel: 1593.

Baigent, Richard Leigh and Henry Lincoln. *The Holy Blood and The Holy Grail.* London: Corgi, 1982.

Bellows, Henry Adams (trans.). *The Poetic Edda: The Mythological Poems* (St.Paul, Minnesota USA: Dover Publications, 2004).

Bond, Frederick Bligh. *The Gate of Remembrance.* Wellingborough: Thorsons, 1918.

Butler, W.E. *The Magician: His Training and Work.* London: Aquarian Press.

Campbell, Joseph. *The Hero with a Thousand Faces.* Princeton U.S.A.: Princeton University Press, 1949.

Carley, James P. *Glastonbury Abbey: The Holy House at the head of the Moors Adventurous.* Glastonbury: Gothic Image, 2006.

Carroll, Lewis. *Lewis Carroll's Diaries Volume 2 January to December 156*. London: Lewis Carroll Society, 1994.
— *The Annotated Alice* (Definitive Edition)—ed. Martin Gardner. London: Penguin, 2001.

Castaneda, Carlos. *Journey to Ixtlan*. London: The Bodley Head, 1972.
— *Tales of Power*. London: Penguin, 1974.

Carey, Ken. *Starseed: The Third Millennium—Living in the Posthistoric World*. San Francisco U.S.A: Harper 1991.

Cavendish, Richard. *King Arthur & The Grail–The Arthurian Legends and their Meaning*. London: Weidenfeld and Nicholson, 1978.

Chardin, Tielhard De. *Future of Man*. London: Fontana 1968.

Conway, D.J. *Animal Magick*. Minnesota: Llewellyn, 1996.

Cooper-Oakley, Isabel. *Masonry and Medieval Mysticism*. London: Theosophical Publishing House, 1900.

Coote, Stephen. *John Keats—A Life*. London: Hodder and Stoughton, 1995.

Dennet, Daniel. *Consciousness Explained*. London: Little Brown, 1991.

Deutsch, David. *The Fabric of Reality*. London: Penguin, 1998.

Dexter, T.F. *Cornwall—The Land of the Gods*. London: Watts & Co., 1932.

Donner, Neal. *Mysticism and the Idea of Freedom*. 1997.

Eliot, T.S. *Collected Poems 1909-1962*. London: Faber and Faber, 1963.
— *Selected Prose*. London: Faber & Faber, 1975.
— *The Waste Land—A Collection of Critical Essays*. London: Macmillan and Co Ltd.,1968.

Eschenbach, Wolfram von. *Parsifal*. London: Penguin, 1980.

Fortune, Dion. *The Mystical Qabalah*. New York, USA: Ibis, 1981.
— Sane Occultism. Loughborough: Aquarian Press, 1987.
— Avalon of the Heart. Wellingborough: Aquarian Press, 1978.

Franz, Marie-Louise Von. *C.G.Jung, His Myths in our Time*. London: Hodder and Stoughton, 1976.

Gettings, Fred. *Dictionary of Astrology*. London: Routledge & Kegan Paul, 1985.

Godwin, Malcolm. *The Holy Grail*. London: Bloomsbury, 1994.

Graddon, Nigel. *Otto Rahn and the Quest for the Holy Grail: The Amazing Life of the Real Indiana Jones*. New York: Adventures Unlimited Press, 2008.

Graves, Robert. *The White Goddess*. London: Faber and Faber, 1961.

Gray, William G. *The Outlook on our Western Way*. New York: Samuel Weiser, 1980.

Greene, Brian. *The Fabric of the Cosmos: Space, Time, and the Texture of Reality*. New York: Kopf, 2004.

Grigsby, John. *Warriors of the Wasteland*. London: Watkins Publishing, 2002.

Grof, Stanislav. *Transpersonal Vision*, London: Sounds True, 1998.

Hancock, Graham. *The Sign and the Seal, The Quest for the Lost Ark of the Covenant*. London: William Heinemann, 1993.

Harding, Elizabeth. *Women's Mysteries*. New York: Rider, 1971.

Hartley, Christine. *The Western Mystery Tradition*. Wellingborough, Northants: Aquarian Press, 1986.

Heraclitus. *Fragment*. New York: Penguin, 2003.

Hume, David. *On Human Nature and Understanding.* London: Collier, 1962.

Hutton, Ronald. *Witches, Druids and King Arthur.* London: Hambledon, 2006.

Kaku, Michio. *Parallel Worlds.* London: Penguin, 2005.

Knight, Gareth. *The Secret Tradition in Arthurian Legend.* Wellingborough: Aquarian Press, 1984.

James, William. *The Varieties of Religious Experience.* London: Collier-MacMillan, 1961.

Jarry, Alfred. *Gestes Et Opinions du Docteur Faustroll Pataphysicien.* London: Methuen, 1927.

Jeans, Sir James. *The Mysterious Universe.* Cambridge: The University Press, 1932.

Jones, Kathy. *In the Nature of Avalon—Goddess Pilgrimages in Glastonbury's Sacred Landscape.* Ariadne Publications.

Jung, Emma, and Von Franz, Marie-Louise. *The Grail Legend.* Princeton: Princeton University Press, 1998.

Laplace. *Essai philosophique Sur les Probabilities.* Tr. F. Wilson Truscott, F. Lincoln Emory. New York: Dover Publications, 1951.

Leisegang, Hans. *Die Gnosis.* Leipzig: 1924.

Loomis, Roger Sherman. *Celtic Myth and Arthurian Romance.* New York: Columbia University Press, 1927.
— *The Grail from Celtic Myth to Christian.* London: Constable 1963.

Malory, Sir Thomas. *The Death of King Arthur.* London: Penguin, 1995.

Mann, Nicholas R. *Energy Secrets of Glastonbury Tor.* Glastonbury: Green Magic, 2004.

Masters, Robert E.L. and Jean Houston. *Psychedelic Art.* New York: Grove Press, 1968.

Matthews, John, and Caitlin. *An Encyclopedia of Myth and Legend— British and Irish Mythology.* London: Diamond Books, 1995.

Michell, John. *The Flying Saucer Vision.* London: Sidgwick and Jackson Ltd., 1967.
— *The New View Over Atlantis.* London: Thames and Hudson, 1983.
— *Confessions of a Radical Traditionalist.* Vermont: Dominion, 2005.

Morris, John. *The Age of Arthur: A History of the British Isles from 350 to 650.* London: Weidenfeld and Nicholson, 1973.

Murray, Muz. *Sharing the Quest.* Shaftsbury, Dorset: Element Books, 1986.

Papus, *The Tarot of the Bohemians.* Los Angeles: Melvin Powers Wilshire Book Company.

Planck, Max. *Eight Lectures on Theoretical Physics.* London: Dover Publications, 1997.

Regardie, Israel. *The Middle Pillar.* Minnesota: Llewellyn, 1970.

Rhan, Otto. *Crusade Against the Grail.* Rochester, Vermont: Inner Traditions, 2006.

Richardson, Alan. *Magical Kabbalah.* Loughborough: Thoth Publications, 2006.
— *The Old Sod—The Odd Life and Inner Work of William G. Gray.* London: Ignotus, 2003.
— *Priestess—The Life and Magic of Dion Fortune.* Wellingborough: Aquarian Press, 1987.
— *Magical Gateways.* Minnesota: Llewellyn Publications, 1992.

Ross, Anne. *Pagan Celtic Britain*. London: Routledge & Kegan Paul, 1967.

Schopenhauer, Arthur. *The World as Will and Representation Vol I*. St. Paul, Minnesota: Dover Publications, 1961.

Stewart, Dr. Thomas Milton. *The Symbolism of the Gods of the Egyptians*. London: A Lewis (Masonic Publishers) Ltd., 1978.

Stevens, Jay. *Storming Heaven*. New York: Grove Press, 1987.

The Anglo-Saxon World—An Anthology. Oxford O.U.P., 1982.

The Diaries of Franz Kafka. Edited by Max Brod. London: Penguin, 1972.

The Mabinogion. Trans. Jeffrey Gautz. London: Penguin, 1976.

The Vulgate Cycle—Queste del Saint Graal. London: Penguin Classics, 2004.

Tomberg, Valentin. *Meditations on the Tarot—A Journey into Christian Hermeticism*. New York: Putnam, 2003.

Wolf, Fred Alan. *Parallel Universes*. New York: Simon and Schuster, 1988.

Woolf, Virginia. *Hyde Park Gate News* (Modern Fiction). London: Hesperus Books, 2006.

Yeats, W.B. *The Celtic Twilight—Myth, Fantasy and Folklore*. Dorset: Prism Press Dorset, 1999.

Zagier, Donald, et al. *The 1-2-3 of Modular Forms*. Berlin: Springer-Verlag, 2008.

Articles/Journals

Leary, Timothy. New York Times. Sept. 20, 1966.

Nelson, R.D. et al. Correlations of Continuous Random Data with Major World Events. Princeton, New Jersey, 2002.

O'Brien, Sean. "Straight to Screen." Times Literary Supplement, August 6, 2010.

Richardson, Alan. Unpublished Essay "The Depths of the Lake," 1989.

MORE BY CROSSED CROW BOOKS

Available Titles

Merlin: Master of Magick — by Gordon Strong
The Bones Fall in a Spiral — by Mortellus
Your Star Sign — by Per Henrik Gullfoss
The Complete Book of Spiritual Astrology — by Per Henrik Gullfoss
Icelandic Plant Magic — by Albert Bjorn
The Black Book of Johnathan Knotbristle — by Chris Allaun
A Witch's Book of Terribles — by Wycke Malliway
In the Shadow of Thirteen Moons — by Kimberly Sherman —Cook
Witchcraft Unchained — by Craig Spencer
Wiccan Mysteries — by Raven Grimassi
The Way of Four — by Deborah Lipp
Celtic Tree Mysteries — by Steve Blamires
Star Magic — by Sandra Kynes
Witches' Sabbats and Esbats — by Sandra Kynes
A Spirit Work Primer — by Naag Loki Shivanaath
A Witch's Shadow Magick Compendium — by Raven Digitalis
Flight of the Firebird — by Kenneth Johnson
Witchcraft and the Shamanic Journey — by Kenneth Johnson
Travels Through Middle Earth — by Alaric Albertsson
Craft of the Hedge Witch — by Geraldine Smythe
Be Careful What You Wish For — by Laetitia Latham —Jones
Death's Head — by Blake Malliway
The Wildwood Way — by Cliff Seruntine